James Barr Walker

The Doctrine of the Holy Spirit

Or Philosophy of the Divine Operation in the Redemption of Man

James Barr Walker

The Doctrine of the Holy Spirit
Or Philosophy of the Divine Operation in the Redemption of Man

ISBN/EAN: 9783337077976

Printed in Europe, USA, Canada, Australia, Japan

Cover: Foto ©Lupo / pixelio.de

More available books at **www.hansebooks.com**

THE DOCTRINE

OF

THE HOLY SPIRIT,

OR,

*PHILOSOPHY OF THE DIVINE OPERATION
IN THE REDEMPTION OF MAN.*

BY

REV. JAMES B. WALKER, D.D.,

*Author of "The Living Questions of the Age," "The Philosophy of the Plan
of Salvation," Etc.*

FOURTH EDITION, REVISED AND ENLARGED.

CHICAGO:
S. C. GRIGGS AND COMPANY.
1874.

Entered according to Act of Congress, in the year 1869, by
CHURCH & GOODMAN,
In the Clerk's Office of the District Court of the United States for the Northern District of Illinois.

Entered according to Act of Congress, in the year 1874, by
S. C. GRIGGS & CO.,
In the office of the Librarian of Congress, at Washington.

PRINTED AT THE LAKESIDE PRESS,
Clark and Adams Sts., Chicago.

TO THOSE WHO BELIEVE THAT FORMS AND DISSERTATIONS CONCERNING THE GOSPEL,—

RATHER THAN FAITH AND THE POWER AND SPIRIT OF THE TRUTH, IS PREVALENT IN MANY CHURCHES OF OUR TIMES,—

THESE PAGES ARE RESPECTFULLY DEDICATED BY

THE AUTHOR.

INTRODUCTION.

WITH this closing treatise, the series of books on the Divine wisdom, manifested in the processes of Creation and Redemption, is complete. This last book we think the most important of all; and in connection with the preceding volumes, we hope enough has been done to establish the conviction in the minds of thoughtful readers, that the Work of Creation and Redemption is a unity — one chain of Creative Progress, begun when "The Spirit of God brooded upon the face of the waters," creating formative tendencies in material things, and begetting the first life-germs in the primal universal sea, — completed when humanity was crowned by the birth of Christ, and the Divine image was begotten again in believing souls.

It has been pleasant for the author to follow the processes of the Divine thought, as they have manifested themselves in Nature and Revelation; and to seek in the progressive development of the whole sublime scheme, a true apprehension of the plan and purpose of the Creator.

In this last book we endeavor to give an exposition of the ultimate form and force of the Doctrine of the Holy Spirit. This doctrine is received in some sense by all Christian sects; yet by many, it is very apparent that the truth is held in form rather than in faith; while none of us have had a sufficiently clear and influential conviction of the dependence of man on the vital operation of the Spirit of God.

The Friends or Quakers have, perhaps, had the most scriptural apprehension of the doctrine in its cardinal principles. But even with them sectarian peculiarities have marred the manifestation of the Divine life. More good would have been done, if reform without needless peculiarities had characterized the life and teaching of the Friends and other reformers of the martyr-period in England. If, instead of discarding music, and other social recreations and enjoyments, the early reformers had aimed to reduce them to happy and beneficent uses, then the doctrine which they made prominent, that the influence of the Spirit is essential to all true worship, would have been more generally accepted by sincere Christians, and there would have been less of fallacy to restrain the Divine operation, as the central power in the kingdom of God.

In this treatise we have endeavored to set forth the rational and scriptural exposition of inspired teaching concerning the Comforter, and to exhibit the place of the Divine Spirit in the Godhead, and in the work of Gospel progress.

We do not assume to have presented the subject in such form that other minds may not add or subtract from the matters herein stated. We have done what God enabled us to do: and, grateful for the knowledge that our preceding books have been the means of good to many persons in many lands, we here close our labors on the whole subject, with the hope that this volume may add strength and completeness to the impression of the others, and that each reader may gain a clearer apprehension of the Divine character and the Divine operation.

TO THE READER.

THE first portion of the following treatise may seem to some metaphysical rather than scriptural. This impression will pass away as the reader advances. The views presented are designed to establish the doctrine of the Father, Son and Spirit on a rational and scriptural basis. While they exhibit the subject in a different light, in some respects, from that in which many have been accustomed to view it, the scriptural integrity of the doctrine is maintained,—and maintained, we think, in such form that the reason does not reluctate against it, as it does against the phraseology in which the doctrine of the Trinity has sometimes been expressed in the formulas of the churches.

The treatise presents, we are sure, a true exposition of this doctrine; and especially of the Work of the Spirit in the process of sanctification. We offer it as a contribution designed to promote intelligent faith, and unity of faith among the various denominations of believing people. We do not hope that the views here presented will be at once recognized by every reader as the true exposition of the doctrine of the Spirit; but after mature discussion of the principles herein propounded, we have no doubt that these pages will aid in accomplishing the end for which they have been written — *to glorify the true God, manifested in Christ, and revealed through Christ, by the Holy Spirit.*

In judging of the views upon which he is about to enter, the reader is solicitously desired to refer the adjudication of any doubt that may arise in his mind to the arbitrament of the Word of God, and to "search the scriptures whether these things be so.'

CONTENTS.

CHAPTER I.

THE HOLY SPIRIT IN THE OLD TESTAMENT.

SECT.	PAGE
1.— The mystery of life	17
2.— The doctrine of the Spirit, a peculiarity of the Bible	18
3.— The doctrine as developed in the Mosaic dispensation	20

CHAPTER II.

THE RELATIVE PLACE OF THE SPIRIT AND THE WORD IN THE ECONOMY OF THE DIVINE MIND.

4.— All mind generically the same	23
5.— Self consciousness of the mental constitution	26
6.— The Scripture view of the Logos, or Son of the Divine mind	30
7.— Views of some of the best Christian thinkers in harmony with this exposition	32
8.— Mind manifested only by its Logos, or out-birth	35

SECT.   PAGE

9. — God becomes imminently and effectively personal only in Christ - - - - - - 37
10. — The Holy Spirit uses the personality of Christ in the work of Redemption - - - - 39

CHAPTER III.

THE HOLY SPIRIT IN THE PERSONALITY OF CHRIST.

11. — The humanity of Christ was by the Holy Spirit - 41
12. — The advent of the Spirit upon Christ at His Baptism, and its abiding unity with His humanity - - 42
13. — The Holy Spirit, abiding in Christ, leads Him into and through the temptation - - - - 44
14. — The ministry of Christ, and the manifestation of God in Christ by the Holy Spirit - - - 45
15. — The sacrifice and resurrection of Christ by the Holy Spirit - - - - - - - 47

CHAPTER IV.

THE ENDOWMENT AND SUPERVISION OF THE APOSTLES BY THE HOLY SPIRIT.

16. — The disciples in the Old Testament state, until after the outpouring of the Spirit - - - - 51
17. — Peter's precipitancy and error in acting before the time 53
18. — Christ's choice of the apostles - - - - 55

SECT.		PAGE
19.	Promise of Christ's special presence by the Spirit, in answer to their supplication	56
20.	All essential truth spoken by Christ to be preserved by the suggestion of the Spirit	58
21.	The spiritual sense promised to the apostles	59
22.	Further exposition of the promise that greater light and power would be given by the Spirit after Christ's ascension	62
23.	The endowment of the apostles with special powers and prerogatives	67
24.	The apostles affirm their consciousness of special endowment	70
25.	The Providence of God working together with the Spirit in furthering the gospel by the instrumentality of the apostles	72

CHAPTER V.

THE UNION OF THE WORD AND SPIRIT IN THE PROCESS OF SANCTIFICATION.

26.	Does an increase of light imply an increase of spiritual power?	80
27.	Of the Living Word as a rule of duty	81
28.	Necessity in reason for a perfect rule of human duty	83
29.	A perfect rule of life the only principle of moral progress	86
30.	The truth being given in the life and precept of Christ, the second necessary thing is the work of the Spirit	89

SECT.		PAGE
31.	Rationale of the Spirit's operation in connection with the truth	91
32.	The preceding views illustrated by experience	94
33.	The sum of preceding deductions	95
34.	The union of the Word and Spirit necessary in the process of conviction and sanctification	97
35.	The preceding views accord with the relations of the Word and Spirit, as they exist in both the finite and the Infinite mind	99
36.	The preceding views confirmed by the teaching of the Scriptures	100

CHAPTER VI.

THE WORK OF CHRIST BY THE DIVINE SPIRIT IN THE MINDS OF BELIEVERS.

37.	The two fold office-work of the Spirit	105
38.	The experimental import of the statement that the Spirit shall not speak of Himself	108
39.	By exhibiting Christ the Spirit likewise exhibits the Father to the soul	110
40.	The Spirit witnesses to the truth of Divine Revelation	112
41.	The nature of the Spirit's witness	116
42.	The influence of the Spirit upon the faculties of the mind separately considered	118
43.	The duty of prayer annexed to the doctrine of the Spirit	124

SECT.		PAGE
44.	The conditions upon which the influence of the Holy Spirit is granted	125
45.	Availing prayer is offered to God in the name of Christ	131
46.	The sum of preceding sections	133

CHAPTER VII.

THE WORK OF THE HOLY SPIRIT WITH THE MINDS OF THE IMPENITENT.

47.	Specific work of the Spirit in impenitent minds	138
48.	The promised convictions of the Spirit experienced by those who hear the gospel under spiritual impression	145
49.	The awakening of the lost sinner, and his return to God, as illustrated by the Lord Jesus	149
50.	The son's life at home	152

CHAPTER VIII.

SUPPLEMENTARY.

51.	The promise of the Holy Spirit in answer to prayer is in harmony with the method of the gospel, that grace is bestowed upon one in order that benefit may be conferred upon others	157
52.	The subjects of prayer should be specifically in view of the mind of the suppliant, when he can not personally communicate with them	162

SECT.		PAGE
53.	The miraculous gifts of the Holy Spirit were not the product of the indwelling Spirit, in the ordinary sense	165
54.	"The prayer of faith shall save the sick, * * * and if he have committed sins they shall be forgiven"	170
55.	Was the spiritual endowment imparted by laying on of hands to be transient or permanent in the churches?	174
56.	Recondite laws of human nature connect themselves with this subject	178

APPENDIX - - - - - - - 189

DOCTRINE OF THE HOLY SPIRIT.

CHAPTER I.

THE HOLY SPIRIT IN THE OLD TESTAMENT.

§ 1.— *The mystery of life.*

THERE is mystery connected with spiritual existence which the human mind cannot fathom. This is not only true of spiritual life, but it is true of all life in all its manifestations, and in all the kingdoms of nature. No finite mind can ever know where life begins, or how the life-germ assimilates to itself a material body. We may speculate about questions of this character — we may examine the lowest manifestation of life as it connects itself with the lowest organized being — still the nature of life, and the manner of its union with materiality, no one may know. To know where the inertia of matter ends and the motion of life begins is, and will be for ever, beyond the limit prescribed to the human intellect.

Knowing, then, nothing of the nature of life, and judging of its attributes only by its manifestations, we would approach with becoming reverence the inquiry concerning the attributes and manifestations of the Spirit of God. A consciousness of the limitation of the human understanding should incline the reason to humility, and to examine Revelation with gratitude, hoping that she may there find aid to discern and appreciate the doctrine of the Divine life. It is an important fact, inviting to such examination, that when reason has been aided by revelation to perceive a truth, the accordance of that truth with her own most profound deductions is, to her, a clear testimony, not only of its validity, but likewise of the value of inspired instruction.

§ 2.— *The doctrine of the Spirit, a peculiarity of the Bible.*

The doctrine of the Holy Spirit is one of the distinguishing peculiarities of the Hebrew and

Christian Scriptures. The view given in the Bible of the creative energies of the Spirit of God, and of its place in the scheme of redemption, is diverse from any other form of thought known to the human mind. No religious system, ancient or modern, gives a view in any wise similar to this doctrine, as revealed in the Scriptures. We do not say that a man, by his spirit, did such an act, or that a man's spirit did it. Nor have pagan nations ever talked thus of their gods.* The peculiarity of the phraseology, and the consistency of its development throughout the whole scheme of revelation, will be, to thoughtful minds, a strong testimony for divine guidance in the doctrinal teachings of Moses and of Christ.

In the opening of the eldest Scripture, the Holy Spirit is spoken of personally. (We do not say as a person; but *personally*.) The possessive form of expression in regard to the Father and the Spirit is used; and the life-giving attribute of the Spirit is introduced with the introduction of life. "The Spirit of God brooded

---

* The form of the idea, and the form of phrase, used by Plato and others in speaking of the "*Soul of the world*," are quite diverse.

upon the face of the waters," begetting formative tendencies in things, and initiating life-germs by which the first organic forms were produced in the primæval sea.* Thenceforward, through all the dispensations, the idea of the life-giving Spirit of God is always recognized.

§ 3.—*The doctrine further developed in the Mosaic dispensation.*

Under the Patriarchal dispensation, when God was known only as Creator, the Spirit is spoken of only in its initial, life-giving energy. Under the dispensation of Moses, an advanced development of the doctrine may be recognized. The agency of the Spirit is here more especially connected with the moral life of men, and its attributes are revealed to the human consciousness, as beneficially related to man's weakness and his sin.

In the *middle* and *later* periods of the Old Testament Church, the faith and experience of devout minds, in regard to the Holy Spirit, approximates more nearly to what is known and taught under the new and perfect dispensation. The Divine presence and the Divine Spirit are

---

* See Appendix A—Moses and Geology.

spoken of interchangeably.* The holiness of the Spirit, its renewing and purifying influence, the impartations of joy, strength and courage derived from its presence in the soul, were clearly appreciated by the Psalmists. The identity of a believer's experience under both dispensations is striking and instructive. When David had grossly sinned, so that pardon seemed almost impossible, he prays (Psa. li). "Create in me a clean heart, O God; and renew a right spirit within me. Cast me not away from thy presence; and take not thy Holy Spirit from me. Restore unto me the joy of thy salvation; and uphold me with thy free Spirit. Then will I teach transgressors thy ways; and sinners shall be converted unto thee." The consciousness of every believer, penitent for some past offence, is almost a reproduction of the state of mind deliniated in these passages.

The prophets of the old dispensation were conscious of the influence of the Holy Spirit, and that all advance in the kingdom of God was gained by its operation. Isa. lxi, 1—"The Spirit of the Lord God is upon me; because the Lord hath anointed me to preach good tidings unto

---

* Psalm cxxxix, 7. "Whither shall I go from thy Spirit; or whither shall I flee from thy presence?"

the meek; he hath sent me to bind up the broken-hearted, to proclaim liberty to the captives, and the opening of the prison to those in bonds." In their apprehension, moral progress came not by human devices, nor by merely human appliances; Zech. iv, 6 — "Not by might, nor by power, but by my Spirit, saith the Lord."

Thus the germ-thoughts of the doctrine of the Spirit lie embedded in the Old Testament. A life-giving agent under the dispensation of Creation, or the Patriarchal — a renewing and purifying power under the legal or Mosaic dispensation. But still, in both, whether under the dispensation of creation, or the more advanced dispensation of law, there is found the *peculiar personal phraseology* which distinguishes the doctrine throughout the whole Scriptures.

As light increases throughout the three dispensations, this germ-truth is further developed — from the blade (the sprout) into the ear, and, under the New Testament, to the full corn in the ear. Yet in all, and through all, there is the same Spirit of God, which vivified the first organic germs, energizing in all modifications of life, and finally renewing, purifying, and guiding those who by faith became obedient to Christ, as "God manifest in the flesh."

CHAPTER II.

THE RELATIVE PLACE OF THE SPIRIT AND THE WORD IN THE ECONOMY OF THE DIVINE MIND.

Our views in regard to the work of the Divine Spirit will become more clear and discriminating if we apprehend, in the outset, as fully as we may, the first truths which underlie our subject, both in the economy of mind and in the revealments of the Scriptures.

§ 4.—*All mind generically the same.*

All mind, finite or infinite, must be the same in its elementary characteristics, so far as known to us.* Reason, conscience, will, in all beings, are homogeneous — the same in their nature, whether finite and fallible, or infinite and per-

---

* We do not discuss the question whether God may not have attributes which have no finite analogues in the human soul. The inquiry would be fruitless, and our argument does not require it.

fect. Reason, so far as she sees, accords with the nature of things physical and moral. Her axioms are universal. We know that two and two must be four with God, as they are with men, because the physical universe is constructed upon the principle of mathematical proportion. Right and wrong enter into moral relations as mathematical proportion enters into physical relations. There can be no response in the human soul to the moral administration of God, unless the primary moral convictions of man coincide with conscience or moral judgment in the Divine mind. If moral truth be not the same, when discovered, to all moral beings, then the moral universe is founded upon the principle of discord. Benevolence, or conformity to the law of love, must be the same in its nature in God and in man, else man in becoming benevolent, by faith in Christ, would not come into conformity with the character of God. Knowledge of the Divine mind, therefore, *so far as the Infinite mind can be comprehended by the finite,* must be obtained through the analogy existing between the human and the Divine minds, and the Divine love must be apprehended through the human susceptibility. Man can not obey a law unless he understands it.

He can not know what love is unless he feels it. He can have no sense of the moral duty due to God, unless the obligation of right and wrong is appreciated* alike by the Divine and the human mind.

To make statements concern ng the Divine mind or the Divine character that can not be appropriated in consciousness, nor appreciated by the reason, is to talk in words that can have no more import to the hearer than a description of colors to a man born blind. If it be not irreverent, therefore, we may say, that if God would create a being to know and appreciate His character, it would, from the nature of things, be necessary that that being should be created with rational and moral powers, the same in kind as those which constitute the Divine perfections. Lower, it may be, than the angels—limited in some directions, immature in others, and imperfect in all; yet still a creature created in the

---

* Just as the movements of the physical universe furnish an exhibition of phenomena to which the human mind may apply its perception of proportion, and thus progressively deduce the laws of nature; so the work of God in nature and revelation being given, the human mind can deduce from the first the natural attributes, and from the second, the moral character, of God.

•

moral image of God alone can know and glorify Him.*

We may assume the deduction, then, as a premise, that an insight into the capacities and faculties of the human mind will teach us something of the economy of the Godhead. And if the views thus educed are sanctioned by a clear exposition of the Scriptures, we shall be sure that we have gained knowledge that will aid us to become acquainted with God, and to be at peace with Him.

§ 5.—*Self-consciousness of the mental constitution.*

That mind has, in some sense, a tri-partite constitution, is, to self-knowing men, beyond question.† Few are able to introvert the eye, and scan with clear-seeing discrimination what is re-

---

* See Appendix B — ANTHROPOLOGY.

† Tri-partite, — if we adopt the prevalent philosophy of an "unknowable" substance or essence in which personality and attribute inhere. If we suppose the "I" to be personality or substance, the view given in the text is somewhat modified, but the phraseology is still valid. Conscience and love are states of the "I." Thought is a generation or outbirth of the "I." Will is the act of the "I." The character of thought and will accords with the state of the Ego.

vealed in their own consciousness; and mental science has been so perplexed by the treatises of scholars to whom God has given no original insight, that knowledge of mind has been obscured and hindered, rather than cleared and furthered, by a multitude of well-meaning writers. Holding all these in abeyance, we will look at this subject in common phraseology and in scriptural definitions: assuming as sufficient for our exposition the common view that there is a substratum or substance of mind known to us only by its manifestations. We shall gain the assent of the thoughtful when we say, that in this *unknowable substance* of mind there are two things which stand out clearly in the field of consciousness—diverse in one sense and indivisible in another, yet both inhering in the Father-substance of the soul. These two hypostates, personalities, or manifestations (call them what you will) are *spirit* and *thought*. There is something in the mind apart from thought which is conscious of producing thought; which sees and judges of the character and fitness of the thought produced; which modifies, arranges, and uses thought (or the word) to effect its purposes. It is not any of the laws of mind; it is more than a faculty of mind. It is something that perceives thought, feeling, and faculty, in consciousness, as features and actions are seen in a glass. If we may not call it the substance of mind, we must regard it as a knowing entity, or personality, a thought-producing and thought-using agent. Different in one sense from the conceived *logos*, or word, as the agent is from the object—standing in relation to thought as the observer to the observed—sometimes as the agent to the instrument.

Now this entity, or "I" of the mind, is designated distinctly by the word "spirit" in the Scriptures; and the testimony of consciousness, concerning the relations of spirit and word in the human mind, is set forth as true both of the human and the Divine mind. The place of the *knowing* spirit and the *known* word is thus stated by the apostle (1 Cor. ii, 10), "The spirit searcheth all things, yea, the deep things of God. For what man knoweth the things of a man, save the spirit of man which is in him? even so the things of God knoweth no man, but the Spirit of God."

But while consciousness and the Scriptures give us this ultimate analysis, all know that the inspired writers do not often speak analytically in regard to the place of the Spirit and Word in the Divine mind. They speak of the Father, Son, and Spirit interchangeably, giving Divine attributes to each of them: and in the baptismal formula, the one name contains the three personalities, Father, Son, and Holy Ghost. It should be observed, also, that the Scriptures not only speak of the Word and Spirit interchangeably, but the Spirit in its efficient qualities is spoken of sometimes as the Spirit of the Father, and at other times as the Spirit of the Son.*

Accepting then the testimony of consciousness and the teaching of the Scriptures, as to the personality of the Spirit and the Word, and their place in the economy of mind; and accepting the same authority for deriving a knowledge of the Infinite by analogies drawn from the human mind, we are prepared to inquire further concerning the relations of the Spirit and the Word to each other and their related place and power in the economy of redemption

---

* Isa. lxi, 1,—" The Spirit of Jehovah is upon me; he hath anointed me to preach glad tidings unto the meek," etc, 1 Pet. i, 11,—" The prophets searched what, or what manner of time, the Spirit of Christ which was in them did signify," etc. Gal. iv, 6,—" God hath sent forth the Spirit of his Son into our hearts," etc.

§ 6.—*The Scripture view of the Logos, or Son of the Divine mind.*

The Evangelist John gives the lineage of the Son of God, as Matthew does that of the Son of Man. In Scripture illustration, the Logos, or conceived Word, is born of the Divine mind, as light is born of the sun. Heb. i, 2, 3,—" God hath spoken to us in these last days by his Son, who is the out-shining of his Father's glory, and the real expression of his nature or person." As we know of the existence and nature of the sun only through the medium of its light, so we can know the moral character of God only by the Mediator, Christ Jesus. This analogy is expressly warranted in 2 Cor. iv, 6,—" God, who commanded the light to shine out of darkness, hath shined in our hearts, to give us the light of the knowledge of the glory of God in the face of Jesus Christ."* The Evangelist John gives the fact divested of its figurative form. "In the beginning was the Word, and the Word was

---

* Those who have read the leading theological writers of the past and present centuries, may have noticed that, for the most part, they are so constrained by their theological systems, that they fear to use the inspired analogies common to the apostles and the earliest fathers, on this subject.

with God, and the Word was God. The same was in the beginning with God. All things were made by him; and without him was not any thing made that was made. In him was life; and the life was the light of men." "The Word was made flesh, and dwelt among us."

And it is only by this manifestation in the person of His Son that God is known to men. "No man hath seen God at any time; the only begotten Son, which is in the bosom of the Father, he hath declared him." And in Matt. xi, 27, "All things are delivered unto me of my Father: and no man knoweth the Son, but the Father; neither knoweth any man the Father, save the Son, and he to whomsoever the Son will reveal him." That is, the Father does not reveal the Son, but the Son reveals the Father; and no man knows the Father but by revelation through the Son.

The conceived Word is as old as the Divine mind — "He was in the beginning with God." (The eternally begotten Son of orthodox theology.) But the revealed or manifested Word, in His relations to man, is no older than the time when the Divine mind was manifested by its Logos in creation; subsequently, in the guidance and culture of the Jewish church,* and finally and perfectly by the incarnation in "the Mediator, the man Christ Jesus."

§ 7.— *Views of some of the best Christian thinkers in harmony with this exposition.*

It is difficult to separate selfishness from system and forms. The man who devises the system, and the man who adopts it as *his* system, have both a personal feeling and identification with it; hence they will press their peculiarities until the truth is restrained and constrained by their dogmatic formularies. It often, therefore, comes to pass that the setting forth of scriptural truth concerning the genesis of the Son of God, in the phrase and manner of the scriptures themselves, is feared, by well-meaning persons as an impeachment of the sectarian forms in which their theology is cast. To relieve this habitude of mind, in regard to the present topic, we annote the thoughts of some of the most eminent and pious theologians, ancient and modern.

---

* 1 Cor, x, 4,—"They drank of that spiritual Rock that went with them: and that Rock was Christ." x, 9,—"Neiter let us tempt Christ, as some of them also tempted, and were destroyed of serpents."

Matthew Henry — the best-read in the Bible of all the commentators — has given the inspired conception in his note on the first passage in the Gospel by John. He says:

"The Evangelist in the close of his discourse (v, 18) plainly tells us why he calls Christ the Word of God: — because He is the only begotten Son which is in the bosom of the Father, and has declared Him.

"WORD is two-fold; word conceived, and word uttered.

"(1.) There is the word conceived, that is, *thought*, which is the only immediate product of the soul — all the operations of which are performed by thought, and it is one with the soul. Thus the second person in the Trinity is fitly called the Word, for He is the first begotten of the Father, that eternal Wisdom which Jehovah possessed, *as the soul doth its thought*, 'in the beginning of his way' (Prov. viii, 22). There is nothing we are more sure of than that we think, yet there is nothing we are more in the dark about than how we think. Who can declare the generation of thought in the soul? Surely then the generations and births of the Eternal mind may well be allowed to be great mysteries of godliness, which we can not fathom, while yet we may adore the depth.

"(2.) There is *word* uttered, and that is speech. Thus Christ is the Word, for by Him, 'God hath spoken in these last times unto us' (Heb. i, 2), and has directed us to hear Him. (Matt. xvii, 5.) He has made known God's mind unto us, as a man's word or speech makes known his thought, as far as he pleases, and no farther."

The devout *Baxter* finds in both the human and the Divine mind a trinity of "essentialities," which he calls life-action, understanding, and will—(Potentia-actus, Intellectus, Voluntas). He does not affirm that these principles are all there is of the Trinity, or the Divine personality; yet they are in his opinion the ground of a three-fold, eternal self-action in the Godhead, and likewise the ground of the Divine manifestation in three persons. *See Meth.* vi, c. 2, *and Prac. Works* 19, 21.

Some passages from the Fathers will indicate the mode of expression not uncommon in the earlier ages of the Christian Church.

Clement of Alexandria writes, in his exhortation to the Greeks: "The Divine Logos, the

Christ, was the cause of our being, and well-being also, *for He was in God.* And now this Logos Himself appears to men, the only being that ever partook of both natures, as well that of God as of man, to be the cause of all good to us."

Tertullian says: "The Greeks denominate that Logos which we translate *Word,* and thus our people, for brevity's sake, say — 'In the beginning the Word was with God;' though it would be more proper to say — Reason, since God was not speaking from the beginning, although rational. * * * Considering, therefore, and disposing by His reason, He effected His will by His word, *which thou mayest easily understand by what passes in thyself."* *Tur. ad Prax.* c. v.

Justin the Martyr — the first of the apologists, who stood in immediate connection with the apostles, says: "It is not allowable to think otherwise of the SPIRIT and POWER *which is in* God than that it is the *Logos,* which also is the first-born of God." — *Ap.* ii.

§ 8. — *Mind manifested only by its Logos, or out-birth.*

We can know the character of a spirit only by its words and acts — its logos revealed in words and action. Man may embody his word impersonally, in written language, and send it to all nations who understand the written character. Why then might not the Word of God be made flesh? Why might not God send His Son — the Word, or out-birth of the Divine mind — to become personal in a human nature, so that the true God might be revealed through the flesh to those in the flesh? "Thus God in these last days has spoken to us by his Son."

From the nature of the case such a manifestation was necessary, or man could never know God.* The Scriptures affirm the form of this manifestation in language that is easily understood. "God was in Christ, reconciling the world to himself." Jesus produces reconciliation by revealing the Divine character in ways adapted to our nature and our wants. He said, "I am the *way*, the *truth*, and the *life;* no man can come unto the Father but by me." He is the Mediator — *the Way*. God and man meet together in His person. God comes in on the side of His divinity, and man comes in and meets God through the side of His humanity. *He is the truth* — the Divine character and will

---

* See "God revealed," etc., B. ii, c, 5.

are manifested through Him. "No man knoweth the Father but the Son, and he to whomsoever the Son will reveal him." *He is the Life* — the Spirit of Life was in Him; and He was a life-giving Spirit.

We shall see more distinctly as we go on that it is the *character*, the *nature* of God, thus revealed in Christ, which becomes the element of saving power in the *soul*. The teaching, the life, and the death of Christ, is a true, and full, and final revelation of the Divine thought, and will, and heart, in regard to man; and by faith, which gives this manifestation effect upon the soul, "Christ Jesus, of God, is made unto us wisdom, and righteousness, and sanctification, and redemption." *

§ 9. — *God becomes imminently and effectively personal only in Christ.*

Man is so constituted as a moral being, that obedience and gratitude can be exercised only toward a *personal being* — a being who *consciously* and *voluntarily* does us good. The idea of theologizing skeptics, that man can be grateful to the

* Cor. i, 30.

laws of nature, or to the bread that satisfies his hunger, is preposterous. Man can feel no sense of responsibility or gratitude to something that is "neither personal nor impersonal"* in any comprehensible sense. Obligation, obedience, gratitude, are possible only when founded upon *the character and voluntary acts* of a personal being.

Now it is by the work of Christ that God becomes imminently personal to the soul. The human mind can have an idea of the personality of an invisible spirit only in connection with its history, its life-action.† My life-work gives character to my personality, in the minds of others, after I leave the world. All that other spirits can know or judge of me as a separate person they must get from the will, intellect, and love manifested in my life. So we can know God as a personal being only by His manifestation in the angelic or human nature — a manifestation of heart and will — feeling and action — which the soul may accept by faith as a revelation of the divine nature. The idea of a God every where

---

* See Parkers "Discourses of Religion."

† Hence the Anthropomorphism of all ages and religions, from the beginning to the end of the world.

present at the same time, over and in nature, may be true, but it is *impersonal*, and hence it is abstract and without life to the human soul. In the presence of such an idea of God, man can neither exercise obedience, gratitude, or worship.

§ 10. — *The Holy Spirit uses the personality of Christ in the work of Redemption,*

Hence we are taught that the Holy Spirit, when He comes to the soul, does not speak of Himself — *of His own personality* — but He takes of the things that belong to Christ, and shows them to the believer.* When the soul is conscious of the Divine presence, *it does not recognize two personalities;* because the Spirit comes clothed in the personality of Jesus, and its life is bestowed through the manifestations which God makes of Himself in His Son.

The Holy Spirit gives to the soul by influx through the susceptibility, a newer and higher consciousness of the Divine nature, which is love. But He is not a revealer of new truths, nor an exhibitor of His own personality. When

* John, xvi, 15.

He visits the pious mind, He does not lead that mind to think of Himself, but of Jesus. He takes of the manifestations of the Divine character, made by Christ, and gives them efficacy, by power and love, in the human soul. He comes to us through the Son, baptized in his humanities, as a ray of light takes the hue of the medium through which it passes; and thus He becomes to the soul the Spirit of both the divine and the human, as it was in Christ Jesus. The Son of God manifests the Divine mind; the Spirit of God uses that manifestation to sanctify and save us. Hence Christ and the Spirit are one to the soul, and one in the Church to the end of the dispensation; as He said, "Lo, I am with you alway, even to the end of the world."*

* The ideas of some of the elder divines, as well as the moderns, are strangely confused in regard to the work of the Spirit, and the relation of the Word and the Spirit in the work of redemption. For evidence of this, see text and notes in Archdeacon Hare's "Mission of the Comforter."

CHAPTER III.

THE HOLY SPIRIT IN THE PERSONALITY OF CHRIST.

THAT there was a special connection between the Holy Spirit and the human nature of Christ is plainly and frequently taught in the New Testament. The inspired teaching on this subject can not be easily misunderstood. The creeds of sects have in some instances blinded its expression, but still the true import of Scripture is generally accepted in the churches. In all the parts, and in all the accomplishments of Christ's mission, the Holy Spirit is spoken of as the developing power. When the plain Bible statement is received as authority, the several passages on this subject scarcely need an exposition. We shall therefore give passages, with only such remarks as seem necessary for their historical connection.

§ 11.—*The humanity of Christ was by the Holy Spirit.*

In His humanity, Christ was the "second

Adam;" the second human nature created immediately by the Divine power.* The humanity of Christ, being originated by the life-giving energy of the Holy Ghost, was hence without the taint of transmitted debility or depravity. Therefore it was declared that the Holy Being born of the Virgin should be called the Son of God. In this pure humanity "dwelled the fullness of the Godhead bodily," as the Shekinah dwelled in the tabernacle in the wilderness. John i, 14,— "The Word was made flesh, and tabernacled among us." John ii, 19—21,— "Destroy this temple, and in three days I will raise it up." "He spake of the temple of his body." Thus the Son of God by eternal generation became united with the Son of Man, or the Son of God by earthly generation, and men "beheld his glory; the glory of the only begotten of the Father, full of grace and truth."

§ 12.— *The advent of the Spirit upon Christ at His baptism, and its abiding unity with His humanity.*

"Jesus increased in wisdom and in stature, and in favor both with God and man;" and

---

* See Appendix C — THE SCIENTIFIC FORMULÆ OF THE BIRTH OF CHRIST.

"when he began to be about thirty years of age he came from Galilee to Jordan to be baptized of John; and being baptized, *"the heavens were opened, and the* HOLY GHOST DESCENDED UPON HIM IN BODILY SHAPE, AS A DOVE." The Holy Spirit being now *personally* in Christ, a voice from heaven proclaimed, "This is my beloved Son, in whom I am well pleased."

This descent of the Spirit of God upon Christ, the second Adam, and its *abiding in Him*, was the appointed witness to John of the Messiahship of the Redeemer. Before this manifestation the Baptizer had known Christ as a holy teacher, but not as the Messiah, till God in his presence "anointed him with the Holy Ghost and with power."* "He that sent me to baptize with water," said John, "the same said unto me, *Upon whom thou shalt see the Holy Spirit descending, and* REMAINING, the same is he which baptizeth with the Holy Ghost. And I saw and bare witness that this is the Son of God."†

* Acts x, 38. † John i, 33, 34.

[Words and quotations that are capital or emphatic in the chain of exposition, are often so marked in the text. The reader is desired to mark quoted and emphasized.]

§ 13.— *The Holy Spirit abiding in Christ, leads Him into and through the temptation.*

After the baptism Luke makes record that Jesus, "*being full of the Holy Ghost,*" returned from Jordan, and "*was led by the Spirit* into the wilderness to be tempted of the devil." The Scriptures teach (James i, 13), that God, increate and separate from sense, "can not be tempted;" wherefore, in the order of reason and mercy, "it behooved Christ in all things to be made like unto his brethren, that he might be a merciful and faithful High Priest in things pertaining to God, to make reconciliation for the sins of the people. For in that he himself hath suffered being tempted, he is able to succor them that are tempted."* Hence "a body was prepared" for the Redeemer, that He might be touched through its sympathies with a feeling of our infirmities. By the incarnation, God came into sensitive sympathy with humanity, and invites humanity to come into sympathy with divinity. Thus the Holy Spirit led Christ through a human experience, "he being tempted in all respects as we are, yet without sin."

* Heb. ii, 17, 18.

§ 14.—*The ministry of Christ, and the manifestation of God in Christ, by the Holy Spirit.*

The apostle (1 Peter i, 11) says of the prophets that they "searched what, and what manner of time, the Spirit of Christ which was in them did signify, when it testified beforehand the sufferings of Christ, and the glory that should follow." And this Spirit of Christ which was in them (not "bodily" and "without measure," but inspiringly) spake of the whole ministry of Christ as being developed by the Holy Ghost. In prophetic transport, Isaiah exclaims (lxi, 1), "The Spirit of the Lord God is upon me; because the Lord hath anointed me to preach glad tidings unto the meek; he hath sent me to bind up the broken-hearted, to proclaim liberty to the captives, and the opening of the prison to them that are bound."

In various forms of language the inspired writers of the New Testament, also, instruct us that Christ's ministry—His miracles—His sacrifice—His resurrection, and the subsequent endowment of the apostles, were by the Divine Spirit.

After God had "*anointed him with the Holy*

Ghost and with power*" at His baptism, He returned from His temptation in the wilderness (into which He had been led by the Spirit) "*in the power of the Spirit into Galilee.*" * To the sense of men — His disciples, as well as others — He was *personally present* as a human being, but His claims to the Messiahship, as the Son of God, He predicated upon the statement (John xiv, 10) — "The Father that dwelleth in me," He "speaketh the words," and "doeth the works."

Hence He says (Matt. xii, 28), — "If I cast out devils *by the Spirit of God*, then the kingdom of God is come unto you." So, likewise, He taught that sin against the Son of Man, conceived of by the presence of His human person (in which even His disciples did not clearly discern the indwelling divinity, (John xiv, 9), was pardonable; but those who with malignant mind should sin against the Holy Ghost, manifested by greater light yet to be given, as well as by miracles of mercy and power, of which they were witnesses, "had no forgiveness, neither in this world, nor in that which is to come." †

* Luke iv, 14. † Matt. xii, 22-23.

§ 15.—*The sacrifice and resurrection of Christ by the Holy Spirit.*

The power and the presence of the Holy Spirit is recognized in the chief act of reconciliation — the sacrifice of Christ upon the cross. Hence it is said (Heb. ix, 14), that "the blood of Christ, who *through the Eternal Spirit* offered himself without spot unto God, shall purge your consciences from dead works to serve the living God."

This purifying effect of Christ's sacrifice is the conscious secret of a true faith, which none of the formal worshipers of this day understand. The love of Christ, by the life of the Spirit, is imparted to those who believe in His sufferings for their good. This quickens their conscience, purifies their heart, and gives love-motive to the will, so that formal worship and selfish works cease: their "conscience is purified from dead works," and thenceforth their works are living works, that is, works produced by love to God and men.

After His sacrifice, Christ was "declared to be the Son of God with power, according to the *Spirit of holiness,* by his resurrection from the dead."* "Whom the Jews slew, *God by his Spirit raised up."* And the Apostle Peter, in pregnant sentences, such as he always wrote, teaches us (1 Pet. iii, 18) that Christ has once suffered for sins, the just for the unjust, that He might bring us to God, being put to death in the flesh, but *quickened, or brought to life, by the Spirit*.

Thus "the God of peace brought again our Lord Jesus Christ from the dead,"† and after His resurrection, being assembled together with His disciples, He breathed on them, and said, "Receive ye the Holy Ghost." And "for about the space of forty days, he continued, before his ascension, until he, *by the Holy Ghost*, had given commandments unto the apostles whom he had chosen." ‡

Thus, in all the vicissitudes of the Redeemer's life, in His death, and in His resurrection, THE SCRIPTURES REQUIRE US TO BELIEVE that *His mission and ministry was executed by the power of the Holy Ghost*. In this sense, "God was in Christ reconciling the world unto himself." "In him was LIFE, and that LIFE was the *light* of men." "The first Adam was made

* Rom. i, 4.   † Heb. xiii, 20.   ‡ Acts i, 2.

a living soul, the second a life-giving Spirit,"— the one transmitting animal life — the other spiritual, eternal life. And the work of Christ, which in the days of His flesh was thus actuated by the Holy Ghost, is still administered, and will be to the end of the world, by the same Spirit, and for the accomplishment of the same ends. Since the resurrection, as we shall see, even more efficiently than before, "Christ of God is made unto men wisdom, and righteousness, and sanctification, and redemption."

CHAPTER IV.

THE ENDOWNENT AND SUPERVISION OF THE APOSTLES BY THE HOLY SPIRIT.*

CHRIST having accomplished His personal work in the world, the next step in the process was to endow with the Spirit, and send forth those apostles whom He had chosen, disciplined, and furnished with the truth of the new dispensation. They were to go forth "as sheep among wolves;" but "endued with a spirit and wisdom which their enemies could neither gainsay nor resist." Thus endowed, and trusting in him who had promised to be with them, they went forth joyfully to a life of labor and suffering — but to a labor sustained by the hope, which by faith had become a reality, that they would establish the kingdom of God upon earth, and initiate an order and worship against which the powers of evil could never prevail.

* *Vide* — Preliminary Essay to McKnight on the Epistles.

§ 16.— *The disciples in the Old Testament state, until after the outpouring of the Spirit.*

With some little advance in spiritual insight, the disciples were in the Old Testament state until after Christ's resurrection. Jesus did not design to remove, even in their case, the forms of Old Testament worship, nor the sense of Old Testament obligation, until after His ascension. All the sanctions of duty were drawn from the Old Testament, until the New was inaugurated. The disciples asked nothing in the name of Christ before His sacrifice in the sense that they did afterwards. They had a purified heart, and an obedient will;* but they had not the spiritual consciousness of the new dispensation until after the outpouring of the promised Spirit. As they went to Emmaus, their words to the risen Redeemer not only indicated that they had not apprehended the import and the necessity of His death (a truth which He had plainly indicated to them), but they disclosed very distinctly the secular views which they entertained of His

---

* John xv, 3. — " Now ye are pure through the word which I have spoken unto you," etc.

mission, even after the fact of His crucifixion. Luke xxii, 14–21 — "We had trusted," said they, "that it had been he who should have redeemed Israel."

The prophets did not fully understand the spiritual nature of Christ's sacrifice nor the spiritual character of that glory which was to follow,* and the disciples appear to have remained with like imperfect conceptions of the character and mission of the Redeemer, until they were "endued with power from on high." They said, when they assembled with Him after the resurrection, and before the outpouring of the Holy Spirit, "Lord, wilt thou, at this time, restore the kingdom to Israel?" † The answer of Jesus (as though an exposition at that time would be of but little value to them) gave no solution of their inquiry, but referred them to the outpouring of the Spirit, for which they were to wait at Jerusalem. "Ye shall receive," said He, "the power of the Holy Ghost coming upon you: ‡ and ye shall be witnesses unto me both in Je-

---

* 1 Peter i, 10-12.   † Acts, 1, 6.

‡ The "*power* of the Holy Ghost came upon the disciples." Upon Jesus the Holy Spirit *descended* and *remained* in a *personal* form.

rusalem, and in Judea, and in Samaria, and unto the uttermost parts of the earth. And when he had spoken these words, while they beheld, he was taken up; and a cloud received him out of their sight." * They then returned to Jerusalem to wait, as Christ had commanded them, for "the promise of the Father," which, said He, "ye have heard of me. For John truly baptized with water; but ye shall be *baptized with the Holy Ghost* not many days hence."

§ 17. — *Peter's precipitancy and error in acting before the time.*

Peter was by nature impetuous. He had the temperament of Luther — a temperament which fits a man for great achievements when chastened by great grace. His precipitancy before his "conversion," or spiritual illumination, often led him into mistakes, and sometimes into sin. An error of this kind, as we suppose, occurred while the disciples "waited" at Jerusalem for the advent of the "promised Spirit." The plain intimation in the instruction of Christ is, that nothing was to be done until they should be "baptized with

* Acts i, 8, 9, and 4, 5.

the Holy Ghost and with power." But the sanguine impulses of Peter prompted him, and he prompted the other disciples, to elect a twelfth apostle before the time. They were instructed to await the influence and guidance of the Spirit before they began their work; yet, under the motion of Peter, they elected Matthias to the apostleship. This election without the Spirit did not receive the Divine sanction. Matthias was no doubt a faithful disciple, but Christ, personally, chose His own apostles; and subsequently to this election He chose and endowed Paul, as the twelfth member of the sacred college. He was called miraculously by the voice of Jesus Himself, and received a special commission to "bear the name of Christ before the Gentiles and kings and the children of Israel;" and the badge of suffering was annexed as in the case of the other apostles. Acts ix, 16 — "I will show him how great things he shall suffer for my sake."*

Before noticing the work of the apostles, and their spiritual consciousness, we will now return a moment, and notice their call and appointment, and the promises of enlightenment and guidance given them in the last instructions of the Re-

---

* See Appendix D— PAUL, NOT MATTHIAS, THE TWELFTH APOSTLE.

deemer. We shall see the whole subject more clearly by noticing the import of specific passages. Some repetition will occur by this method, but it will serve to bring out the application of the same thought in different relations.

§ 18.— *Christ's choice of the apostles.*

John xv, 16,—"Ye have not chosen me, but I have chosen you, and ordained you, that ye should go and bring forth fruit, and that your fruit should remain: that whatsoever ye shall ask the Father in my name, he may give it you."

The choice of the apostles and their appointment to their vocation are here stated. Jesus had communicated to them the truth, which He tells them in the context He had "received of the Father." Ver. 15,—"All things that I have heard of my Father I have made known unto you." Hence *from* the Father, *through* the Son, *by* the Spirit, they were endowed for their holy office. As in ver. 26, 27,—"When the Comforter is come, whom I shall send unto you from the Father, even the Spirit of Truth, which proceedeth from the Father, he shall testify of me: and ye shall bear witness because ye have been with me from the beginning." In their subsequent work the apostles understood and affirmed their commission as witnesses conjointly with the Holy Spirit. They said (Acts v, 32), *we are witnesses, and so is also the Holy Ghost*, which God hath given to them that obey Him.

Thus by the instruction of Christ and the endowment of the Spirit they were qualified for their mission. They were to be the seed-men of the dispensation, the fruit of whose lives was to be permanent spiritual instruction in the churches, and for all mankind. In accordance with this appointment, their fruit remains in the inspired writings, and in church organizations; and this truth will ever continue the element of enlightenment and of sanctification to us and to all future generations of men.

§ 19. — *Promise of Christ's special presence by the Spirit, in answer to their supplication.*

In conjunction with the appointment of the apostles, and with the promise that their labors should remain as an abiding blessing to mankind, there is assurance given them that their prayers should be answered. They would need constraint, aid, and guidance in their work, and this was granted according to the same principle that governs other cases, that is, on condition of faith and obedience. But, as their work was to be permanent and special, so corresponding plenary communications were furnished. The promised answer to their prayer had, no doubt, reference, in an especial sense, to the gift of the Holy Spirit, that should live internally in their consciousness, and work externally in the providences that surrounded them. John xiv, 14-18,—"If ye ask any thing in my name, I will do it. If ye love me, keep my commandments. And I will pray the Father, and he shall give you another Comforter, that may abide with you forever; even the Spirit of Truth; whom the world can not receive, because it seeth him not, neither knoweth him :* but ye know him; for he dwelleth with you, and shall be in you." And then,

---

* The world can have no spiritual consciousness of Christ as a Divine Saviour. They can know Him historically, as to His humanity; but it is the Spirit that gives the divine to the idea of His personality. The Son of Man they may know, but not the Son of God. They may know Christ in Matthew, Mark, and Luke, but not in John. "No man can call Jesus Lord, but by the Holy Ghost." Christ in the spirit is by faith; Christ in the letter is by intellect.

identifying Himself with the Holy Spirit, and His second coming with the coming of the Spirit, He says, "*I* WILL not leave you *comfortless, I* WILL come unto you." That is, in the Comforter, Jesus would return as a spiritual Saviour — to comfort them, to be *with* them, and *in* them. *

§ 20.—*All essential truth spoken by Christ to be preserved by the suggestion of the Spirit.*

John xiv, 20, — " But the Comforter, which is the Holy Ghost, whom the Father will send in my name,† he shall teach you all things, and bring all things to your remembrance, whatsoever I have said unto you."

This is a divine guarantee that the communication of truth by the apostles should be perfect. They were to be guided into all truth necessary to the ends of their mission — truth adequate to the enlightenment and sanctification of men. And if, through the imperfection of memory, any ne-

---

* NOTE. — That the Spirit comes in Christ's personality is here distinctly and authoritavely affirmed.

† "Name" is used in the New Testament synonymously with character, nature, or personality.

cessary words had been forgotten; or if, through the imperfection of apprehension, any words had been wrongly construed, the Spirit would suggest the idea in such form and connection that it would be expressed in its true import; albeit in the phraseology peculiar to the character and culture of the apostolic witness. Many volumes may have been spoken by the Saviour in order to convey to the apostles the required ideas, yet nothing necessary for human good in all His teachings was to be lost. The Comforter, by quickening conception, guiding in the law of suggestion, and giving spiritual unction to the soul, would "guide them into all truth."

§ 21.—*The spiritual sense promised to the apostles.*

The apostles, as we have noticed, were in the Old Testament state until after the outpouring of the Spirit. The human person of Christ, too, being before their eyes, shut out, in a sense, "the light of the knowledge of the glory of God," as it subsequently "shone in the face of the Redeemer."* Jesus recognized their want of

---

* 2 Cor. v, 16,—"Yea, though we have known Christ after the flesh yet now, henceforth, know we him (in this sense) no more."

spiritual strength and spiritual insight, and promised them more light and better appreciation after His ascension. And because the spiritual import of His teachings required a sense to which they could not then attain, He often spake to them in parables that might be spiritually construed at the full time. The exposition of these parables He sometimes gave, yet they continued to construe them in the Old Testament sense. Even when they supposed that they understood their teacher, as in John xvi, 29, 30, still they did not perceive; and the import of Christ's replies indicates their continued dullness, and refers them to coming events, that would be evidence to themselves of their misapprehension. "Do ye now believe?"—ye think ye do; but when I shall have been crucified, as I have said, instead of understanding the true state of the case, ye will all be scattered, every man to his own, as if My mission had failed. But notwithstanding their dullness in the presence of His humanity, He promised them, in the future, eyes to see the *spiritual sense*, and ears to hear the words now spoken to them as the words of God. "These things," said He (John xvi, 25), " have I spoken unto you in proverbs: but the time cometh, when

I shall no more speak unto you in proverbs, but shall show you plainly of the Father." That is, they did not now perceive the full import of the words which spoke of His Divinity; but the time was approaching when the Father's character, revealed by Him, would be revealed in their consciousness by the influx of the Holy Spirit. "At that day," He said, "Ye shall know that I am in the Father, and ye in me, and I in you."

This knowledge, which they were to possess after their spiritual illumination, would be through a manifestation of Himself by the Holy Spirit, and in this manifestation all the attributes of the Father would be revealed to them through Him. John xvi, 14, 15,—*The Holy Spirit*, when He is come, "shall glorify me: for he shall receive of mine, and shall show it unto you. *All things that the Father hath are mine:* therefore said I, that he shall receive of mine, and shall show it unto you." Hence, the Saviour said to His disciples in this connection—ye ought to "rejoice that I go to the Father, because the Father is greater than I." That is, the Father sends the Word and is revealed by it. When I depart in the flesh the Spirit will come and give divinity and power to My personality, and thus all the attributes of the Father will be manifested unto you more clearly than ye can now perceive them. This revelation of the Godhead of the Father through the Son would be more full and clear after the advent of the Spirit; not only because the Spirit was veiled and localized in a sense in Christ's humanity,* but because when the Word returned to the bosom of the Father, having revealed by the crucifixion the perfect love of the Godhead, then by the Spirit, in the personality of Christ, the Father would be revealed in love both by Word and Spirit to the human soul.

§ 22.—*Further exposition of the promise that greater light and power would be given by the Spirit after Christ's ascension.*

There are plain passages† in which Christ teaches that the Spirit could not be given to the world, in its plenitude and perfection, until He had finished His work on earth and ascended to heaven. Guided by the Scriptures, we can see reasons for the statements which promise this in-

---

* See Hare's " Mission of the Comforter." Notes.
† Luke xxiv, 49; John xiv, 12, 16; and xvi, 7, 13.

crease of spiritual power. The great sacrifice was not yet offered. This was a revelation of Divine love more perfect than had before been manifested on earth; the Spirit, therefore, who was not to speak of Himself, but to use the spiritual material furnished by the Redeemer, had truth in more plenitude, and could make clearer manifestations of Divine love after than before the crucifixion.

Besides this, the resurrection and ascension of Christ were evidences that His work had been accepted of the Father. When there was evidence that the Father raised Jesus from the dead, then in the minds of all those who believed the fact, the rejection of Christ would produce a sense of sin against God. The resurrection of Christ from the dead was absolute evidence that God approved and authorized His work; hence the Spirit, by the resurrection, would not only reveal greater love by the sacrifice of Christ to those who received Him,[*] but greater guilt in those who had rejected Him. In view of this, Jesus said, "When the Comforter shall come, he will convince the world of righteousness, because I go to the Father." My teaching, having re-

---

[*] 1 Peter 1, 3.

ceived visibly the sanction of the Father, will become the rule of righteousness by which men will be convicted of sin.

These manifestations, to be used by the Spirit thenceforward, were powers existing after the fact that did not exist before, except imperfectly in type and shadow. Hence *greater spiritual power* was promised to attend, and did accordingly attend, the preaching of the apostles after the advent of the Spirit, than had accompanied the preaching of Christ before. John xiv, 12,— "Verily, verily, I say unto you, he that believeth on me, the works that I do shall he do also; and greater works than these shall he do; because I go unto my Father."

The apostles likewise, after they were "converted," as Peter needed to be, into the spiritual dispensation,* taught that the promises of Christ, in regard to the plenitude of life by the Spirit, did not refer to the days of His flesh, but to the greater work, in a spiritual sense, which would be accomplished after His ascension. John vii, 37–39,—"In the last day, that great day of the feast, Jesus stood and cried, saying, If any

* Are not many men of our day still partly in the Old Testament State?

man thirst, let him come unto me, and drink. He that believeth on me as the Scripture hath said, out of his heart shall flow rivers of living water." But this did not have its full import that day, nor did it find its true verification until the advent of the Spirit. The apostle therefore adds, as an exposition of the words, "But this spake he of the Spirit, which they that believe on him should receive: *for the Holy Ghost was not yet given; because that Jesus was not yet glorified.*"

When we add to these thoughts the fact already alluded to, that Christ, as the Son of Man, could be personally present in one place only at the same time, but the Spirit would, after its advent, be an everywhere-present revealer of Christ—then the greater glory to be manifested after the days of Christ's ministry is clearly apparent. The words of Christ then became "spirit and life" to those who believed, and all the efficacy contained in a perfect revelation of the Divine character which had been given by the mission of Christ, was used to quicken and sanctify the human soul.

"It was expedient," therefore, after the truth had been perfectly revealed, and the material of sanctification fully provided, that Christ, in His humanity, "should go away," in order that by His spiritual presence He might be every where present with each disciple and with His churches, until the end of the world. After the ascension, therefore, the presence of the Spirit is spoken of as Christ's own presence. "Wherever two or three are gathered together in my name, there I am in the midst of them;" and "Lo! I am with you always, unto the end of the world."

According to the foregoing exposition, while the physical power of miracles* was manifested, perhaps, in a less degree after the ascension of Christ than before, the spiritual power of truth in the souls of men was in all senses greatly

---

* It cannot be questioned that miracles were necessary to moral progress in the time of Christ. No truth, as from God, could have been received without them. All men believed that their divinities granted power to their votaries to work miracles. Either the new religion must be introduced by miracles, or God must, by miracle, destroy the conviction in all minds that miracles could be wrought. In that age a miracle was the only means of connecting the authority of God with truth. I must believe the facts stated as miracles, but *how the effects were produced*, whether *subjectively* in the minds of the witnesses — whether in accordance with, or by control of natural laws is not important. *The* EFFECT of the miracle, not the form, *was the necessity*. [See Phil. of Plan of Salvation, Chapter iii.]

increased. At the advent of the Spirit, on the day of Pentecost, a mighty work of love and power began in the world, the energy and glory of which will not end until the "kingdoms of this world shall become the kingdoms of our Lord and his Christ, and he shall reign for ever and ever."

§ 23.— *The endowment of the apostles with special powers and prerogatives.*

After the Redeemer had, "*by the Holy Ghost, given commandments to his apostles,*" immediately previous to His ascension, He gave them their commission, accompanied by the promise of His presence and supervision in the great endeavor to bring the world to believe in Him as the manifestation of the true God —"Go ye therefore and teach all nations, baptizing them into the [one] name* of the Father, the Son, and the Holy Ghost; teaching them to observe all things whatsoever I have commanded you; and

---

* The "*one* name," including all the attributes and qualities of the three personalities, the Father, Son, Holy Ghost. By one conception of our finite minds we cannot compass God in all His relations to us. God is what the *three conceptions* — Father — Son — Holy Spirit, united, reveal Him to be.

lo! I am with you always, even unto the end of the dispensation."

At the appointed time and place, the promise that they should be endowed for their work by a supernatural manifestation of the Holy Spirit was fulfilled. Acts ii, 1–4 — "When the day of Pentecost was fully come, they were all with one accord in one place. And suddenly there came a sound from Heaven as of a rushing mighty wind, and it filled the house where they were sitting. And there appeared unto them cloven tongues like as of fire, and it sat upon each of them. And they were *all filled with the Holy Ghost*, and began to speak with tongues as the spirit gave them utterance." When thus "baptized with the Holy Ghost," they were at once endowed with impulse, courage, and spiritual insight, which they did not possess before; and it may be that the tongues that sat upon them gave their thoughts articulation on this special occasion, so that the strangers from foreign cities present in Jerusalem, each heard the speaker's thoughts enunciated in his own language. Hence immediate and immense impression was produced. The work of the world's regeneration was begun. Many priests and people of

Jerusalem, together with a multitude from foreign cities, became subject to the faith. The supreme council of the nation was agitated and divided, and there was neither policy nor power that could suppress the progress of the new life.

The apostles, before dull and literal in their sense, had now a clear apprehension of the spiritual nature of Christ's mission, and of the approaching dissolution of the local and imperfect* ritual of Moses. For declaring the abrogation of the Mosaic economy, Stephen was put to death, as his Maste had been before, by the malice of the rulers. The witnesses suborned against him said (Acts vi, 13, 14), "This man ceaseth not to speak blasphemous words against this holy place, and the law: for we have heard him say, that this Jesus of Nazareth shall destroy this place, and change the rites which Moses delivered us."

The apostles were thus evidently endowed not only with an understanding of the spiritual mission of Christ, but likewise with a knowledge in some respects of the future purposes of God,

---

* "Imperfect," not in its adaptation to its place and work as an introductory dispensation, but imperfect in light, love, and righteousness. "Grace and truth are by Jesus Christ."

although they may not have known the form nor the precise time in which those purposes would be accomplished. When, therefore, the Gospel had been preached, " first at Jerusalem, and Judea, and Samaria," the disciples were, by persecution, " scattered abroad," in order that the truth they taught might be carried " to the ends of the earth." Saul of Tarsus, who had held the clothes of those who stoned Stephen, was converted. The college of apostles was complete. The partition wall between the Jews and Gentiles, as indicated to Peter in a vision, was broken down, and the streams of Gospel light and life flowed out to the Gentiles.

§ 24.—*The apostles affirm their consciousness of special endowment.*

The apostles constantly claimed that God by His Spirit was present in their endeavors. Hence the sin of Ananias and Sapphira was declared to be sin against the Spirit of God. They "*preached the Gospel with the Holy Ghost sent down from heaven;*" and claimed distinctly to speak by inspiration of the Spirit. 1 Cor. ii, 12, 13,—" Now we have received, not the spirit of the world, but the spirit that is of God; that we might know the things that are freely given to us of God. Which things also we speak, not in the words which man's wisdom teacheth, *but which the Holy Ghost teacheth;* comparing spiritual things with spiritual." They understood, likewise, the doctrine propounded in the preceding sections. The Holy Spirit in their minds was the same as Christ in them. "*It pleased God,*" says Paul (Gal. i, 16), "*to reveal his Son in me*, that I might preach him among the Gentiles."* To those whom they ordained, they said (2 Tim. i, 14), "That good thing which was committed unto thee, keep by the Holy Ghost which dwelleth in us." By the laying on of hands,† *by those who possessed the Spirit*, they claimed that the Spirit was communicated to others. And in addressing the epistles to the

---

* A revelation of Christ in the soul by the Spirit was necessary in the early period in order to preach the gospel; should it not be so in all periods of the church?

† The doctrine of the laying on of hands will be better understood hereafter. When the power of the Holy Spirit energizes in the souls of administrators, its communication to others will be more apparent than it ordinarily is in the present age. Apostolic succession is by the Holy Spirit. Laying on of hands in this sense is a cardinal doctrine (Heb. vi, 2).

seven churches of Asia, and through them to the churches in later ages, it is written, "Hear what the Spirit saith unto the churches."

Thus, the internal consciousness of the apostles was true to the external manifestation. "The Holy Ghost was witness for them;" while they accomplished their work "by signs and wonders, and divers miracles, and gifts of the Holy Ghost, according to his will."*

§ 25. — *The providence of God working together with the Spirit in furthering the Gospel by the instrumentality of the apostles.*

It has been shown, we think beyond doubt, in the preceding chapters of this series of books, that the Divine energy, operating through all ages and dispensations, wrought to an end foreseen from the beginning; that God is accomplishing a plan in the earth, established upon fixed principles and developed by fixed laws; a plan which unites the kingdoms of nature with each other — the physical with the moral; a plan which extends itself from the form and propor-

---

* Heb. ii, 4.

tions of the original atoms of matter, onward to the moral creation in man; and onward still until it shall ultimate in a perfect physical and moral condition beyond the present.* Jesus said, "My Father worketh hitherto, and I work." I came "to finish the work which the Father hath given me to do"—*i. e.*, to fulfill the ritual of Moses, put an end to its burdens, and develop its limited economy into the final spiritual dispensation of Father, Son, and Holy Ghost.

Hence the Divine Providence and the Divine Spirit were co-workers in the spread of the gospel.† Events so transpired, by Divine interposition, that the knowledge of truth was advanced, whether the providence, in a temporal sense, was propitious or otherwise. The apostles became witnesses at Jerusalem, at Samaria, and to the Gentiles. When their work was done at Jerusalem they were, by the providence of God, dis-

---

* See "God revealed in the Process of Creation, and by the Manifestation of Christ."— BOOK I.

† When Jesus commissioned His disciples and sent them forth to preach the gospel, He said, "All power in heaven and on earth is given unto me." And those who have eyes to see can discern the providence of God working with the truth of the gospel in producing the moral progress of the race.

persed throughout Judea and Asia Minor. Saul aided to banish and scatter the witnesses, and thus, as a persecutor, his agency was overruled to accomplish the same object which he afterwards voluntarily accomplished as an apostle. When the work was mostly done with the Jews, the case of Cornelius, and other like incidents, introduced thoughtful Gentiles into the gospel kingdom. Even the honest difference of Paul and Barnabas—who, *by the dictation of the Spirit*, had been sent out as missionaries from the Church at Antioch—was made a means of disseminating more widely the truth among both Jews and Gentiles in Europe and Asia. The public trials of the apostles before magistrates, and their providential deliverances, tended to the same end. In such cases provision was made for their special guidance; and they were instructed to depend on the interposition by the Spirit in their minds. Mark xiii, 11,—" Take no thought beforehand, neither premeditate :* but whatsoever shall be given you in that hour, that speak ye : for

---

* The law of suggestion is so compact in men of cold temperament and wary mind,—thought is so collated by caution and premeditation, that there seems often no room for even the Holy Spirit to interpose a suggestion.

it is not you that speak, *but the Holy Ghost.*" Hence, by natural and connected incidents, in which the blind could see no providence, Paul was brought before the rulers at Jerusalem, at Cæsarea, in the Islands of the Sea, at Rome; all in accordance with the pre-statement in his commission, in regard to the class before which he should testify, and the manner in which, during his ministry, he should glorify God.

In the imprisonments of the apostle, too, the design of God was especially propitious. The most precious treatises, inspired and uninspired, which the Church possesses, have been written in prison. We could not do without the Epistle to the Philippians, nor that to Timothy. Nor could we well spare the "Pilgrim's Progress," nor the prison thoughts of Penn, Baxter, and other holy men of the modern age. The devil, by casting saints into prison,* has aided to cast himself out of the Church of God. Evil is made subservient to ultimate good.

But not only in regard to the general move-

---

* Rev. ii, 10, 11,—"Fear none of those things which thou shalt suffer. Behold the devil shall cast some of you into prison, and ye shall have tribulation ten days. Be thou faithful unto death and I will give thee a crown of life."

ments of the apostles in the cities and nations of the Old World, but likewise in the time and direction of their travels, and in their personal efforts for the conversion of individuals, the providence and Spirit of Christ combined to guide their agency. If they devised plans contrary to the Divine plan, they were prevented from fulfilling them. Acts xvi, 6 — "When Paul and Timothy had gone through Phrygia and the region of Galatia, and were *forbidden of the Holy Ghost* to preach the Word in Asia, after they were come to Mysia, *they essayed to go into Bythinia:* but *the Holy Spirit suffered them not.*" The gospel had been offered and urged in Asia so far as the preparation of the people and the justice and mercy of God at that time required; hence they were directed by a vision to go over into Europe, and help the few who labored to promote gospel interests in Macedonia.

It was the Spirit (Acts xi, 12) that bade Peter visit the Roman officer at Cæsarea, and in order that the gospel might be carried into Ethiopia, "*the Spirit* said unto Philip," (Acts viii, 29), "Go near to the chariot of the Eunuch," who, as he traveled, read in the prophecies of Isaiah (liii, 7, 8) — a passage foreshadowing the sacrifice of Christ. The disciple thus sent by the Spirit was invited into the conveyance. The Eunuch was instructed and baptized, and carried the gospel in his heart into the midst of Ethiopia. The appointed work of the deacon being thus done, the "*Spirit caught away Philip*, who was found at Azotus; and passing through, he preached in all the cities until he came to Cæsarea."

Thus "filled with the Spirit," and guided by providence, the apostles of Christ fulfilled their mission;—preaching the gospel of the kingdom in "*demonstration of the Spirit*, and with power;" gathering churches; "ordaining elders in every city;" and writing letters to guide the life and perfect the work of righteousness in the minds of believers. The summing-up of their life-labor, as it stood related to God and men, is striking and instructive. 2 Cor. vi, 4–10,—" In all things approving ourselves as the ministers of God, in much patience, in afflictions, in necessities, in distresses, in stripes, in imprisonments, in tumults, in labors, in watchings, in fastings;—by pureness, by knowledge, by long suffering, by kindness, by the Holy Ghost, by love unfeigned, by the word of truth, by the power of God, by the armor of righteousness on the right hand and on the left, by honor and dishonor, by evil report and good report; — as deceivers, and yet true; as unknown, and yet well known; as dying, and behold we live; as chastened,. and not killed, as sorrowful, yet alway rejoicing; as poor, yet making many rich: as having nothing, and yet possessing all things."

Behold how the commissioned apostles of Jesus Christ "fought the good fight of faith," until they "finished their course," sealed their testimony with their blood, and departed to be with Christ. They rest from their labors, but their fruit remaineth. "Being dead, they yet speak," and their words are still rendered efficacious by the power of the Holy Ghost to enlighten and sanctify the souls of men; and those who have ears to hear still hear them preaching " CHRIST CRUCIFIED; THE POWER OF GOD, AND THE WISDOM OF GOD, TO THE SALVATION OF EVERY ONE THAT BELIEVETH.

CHAPTER V.

THE UNION OF THE WORD AND SPIRIT IN THE PROCESS OF SANCTIFICATION.

We have seen that Christ revealed the rule of human duty, both in precept and example, and that no rule of life for men can be perfect without both of these.* And having given the rule and manifested perfectly the Divine character, in closing His mission, He promised that after His ascension "the Holy Spirit, which proceedeth from the Father," would be given, through Him, to lead the chosen witnesses into all truth, and to endow them with spiritual insight, and power from on high. And in this the great promise was fulfilled, that He would be with them until the end of the world, to supervise and to sustain them in their work. We have seen these promises accomplished in the conscious experience

---

* See "Philosophy of Plan of Salvation," chap. x.

of the apostles, and by the providence and the spiritual power connected with their mission. They went every where "preaching the gospel with the Holy Ghost sent down from heaven." We come now to inquire concerning the relations of the Word and Spirit in the work of human salvation.

§ 26.—*Does an increase of light imply an increase of spiritual power?*

Man, in order to eternal life, needs two things, —Truth and Love,—Light and Life,—Word and Spirit. Christ came a light into the world, revealing a standard of life which was above the natural; and to which, therefore, the natural mind was apathetic and averse.* Perhaps this "higher law" implied an advanced dispensation of the Spirit, in order that man might be able to appreciate and obey it. Hence, in order to conformity to the new standard of duty, man is to be "born again from above." He becomes "a new creature in Christ Jesus," who is the head of a new species of humanity. The germs of all

* "That which is born of the flesh, is flesh"—"is of the earth, earthy."

new species are by Divine interposition. Hence the income of the Word and the Spirit would be in the order of the Divine working, and according to the law of progressive development.

However this may be best stated, it is an admitted truth, that with the increased light of the Word, which required a higher attainment in moral excellency, there came, at the same time, increased life and strength by the Holy Spirit.

Let us look, then, at the related offices of the Word and Spirit as revealed in the Scriptures. We will consider them first separately, that we may the better understand their relations to each other, and the necessity of their union in the work of redemption.

§ 27.— *Of the Living Word as a rule of duty.*

We assume again, what has been elsewhere shown,* that precept and example combined is the only perfect form of instruction; and that example, in order to be a rule of duty adapted to human beings, must be *a human example;* because men could not follow the example of an

---

* Philosophy of Plan of Salvation, chap. x.

angel, nor of any nature different from their own.

Now the apostles understood the necessity of the incarnation in this respect. Christ's character, manifested by His life, was the model into which they sought to mould humanity. He was "the mark of the prize of the high calling" to which they struggled to attain, while they invited others to the same endeavor.

Jesus said (John xvii, 18, 19), "As the Father hath sent me into the world, even so have I also sent them into the world. And for their sakes I sanctify myself, that they also might be sanctified, through the truth." And referring, no doubt, to this principle — perhaps to this expression — the author of the letter to the Hebrews says (ii, 10, 11), "For it became him, for whom are all things, and by whom are all things, in bringing many sons unto glory, to make the captain of their salvation perfect through suffering. For both he that sanctifieth and they who are sanctified are all of one; for which cause he is not ashamed to call them brethren." That is, Christ assumed a sanctified humanity in order that His followers might be sanctified by conformity to His image. Hence He was "not ashamed to call them brethren." They were, by assimilation to His life and spirit, raised from the sphere of the earthly, mortal, Adamic species, into the sphere of a new spiritual life, of which Christ was Himself the head and elder brother.

§ 28.—*Necessity in reason for a perfect rule of human duty.*

There is a reason in the nature of man requiring the revelation of a perfect rule of duty. It is not only true that man had lost the knowledge of both the true God and the true man, and could therefore settle no rule of duty for himself in regard to either; but it is further true, that in the absence of a perfect rule of righteousness, and often in its presence, there is that in man which leads him to establish for himself an imperfect standard of life. Man, by an impulse of his nature, always measures himself by some standard of character, and judges himself thereby, and the main difficulty which hinders moral progress is, that men are prone to measure themselves by standards that will produce within them a sense of self-complacency rather than of conviction of sin. Even malefactors, who live in communities, have a standard of character among themselves by which they seek and obtain honor one of another. And from the outlaw up to the moral citizen of good natural qualities, each one has some ideal standard by which he judges of himself. The moralist usually compares himself with some professor of religion, whose character he deems to be no better, or even worse than his own. This comparison gives him a feeling of ease and self-complacency. Instead of stimulating, it prevents moral progress. Hence the more moral the character of any one may be who does not receive Christ as the standard by which he judges himself, the more difficult it will be for him to have a sense of sin and of personal unworthiness. His measurement of himself by the life of other imperfect persons produces a spirit just the opposite of that which he should possess, and which he would possess if he measured himself by the Divine standard of human character. If he measured his character, and judged his motives by the unselfish life of Jesus, he would see his sinfulness and feel contrite and penitent; but measuring himself by false and imperfect standards, he deceives himself, and must remain unhumbled and self-justified. Men are often unconscious of the fact; but the disposition "to measure themselves by themselves" is natural to every human mind. And every one who thus estimates his own moral character by a comparison with others, will remain self-justified and self-deceived until he dies.

And not only the unprofessing world, but the professed followers of Christ, by "measuring themselves among themselves, and comparing themselves by themselves, are not wise." They satisfy themselves with the forms of piety, while they possess neither gospel faith nor gospel practice. They justify their own sin by the sin of some other, and thus accumulate the sins of many others in their own character. This is unwise and wicked. A false standard of judgment necessarily causes men to form a false estimate of themselves. Paul said he dare not be of the number who thus deceived themselves; nor would he compare himself with any standard except "the measure of the rule which Christ had extended to him."

Now in Christ a true rule of duty is provided, by which if any man measure himself, he will see his character as it really is in the sight of God. If a carpenter were to measure his work by a false rule, when a true one was offered and urged upon him, he would be at the same time a fool and a sinner; and in the end both he and his work would be condemned. So all individuals who measure themselves and judge of themselves by a false moral standard, in the presence of the true one, must be condemned when the true rule of judgment is applied to the work of their life. To meet this appetency of the mind, the Divine standard in the example and precept of Christ is provided, and, whether we are willing to judge ourselves by it or not, God will judge us by it. A government does not judge men by their own factitious standards, but always by its own published rule of duty. So God will judge the world by Jesus Christ.* " The words which he has spoken unto us will judge us at the last day." †

§ 29.—*A perfect rule of life the only principle of moral progress.*

A perfect standard of life and motive, in the light of which men may see their moral delinquencies, is a necessity in moral government. It

---

* Acts xvii, 31. † John xii, 48.

is one of the essential requisites by which alone moral progress can be promoted among men. A sense of present imperfection is an absolute prerequisite to moral advancement. A man can have no impulse from his conscience or his reason to go forward to higher moral attainments unless he *sees* and *feels* present deficiencies in himself; and this he can see only in the light of a standard that is above his present character, and by which his present condition is condemned; while he is at the same time invited and encouraged to rise to a higher sphere of life.

And, furthermore, in order to the perfection of moral beings, this standard must be such a one, that while it approves and stimulates the upward effort, yet it is not attained at any point short of moral completeness of human character. Whenever the soul reaches a point that there is no standard to convict it of imperfection, its further attainment is impossible, because conscience and reason, instead of prompting it forward, would require its quiescence in its present moral condition.* Hence, until men are "holy as God is

---

* Thus Pagan nations, as China and India, have made no progress for a thousand years. They can not rise above their standards. Christian nations will make constant progress, be-

holy," the character of Christ will furnish a standard that will convict them of sin, and thus give impulse to moral progress.

Upon this "mark of the prize of the high calling of God in Christ Jesus" the Christian fixes his eye; and as he advances he finds Christ ever before him. In the light of a perfect example he sees his defects in motive, in practice, and in spirit; and yet the infinite love of the Divine Guide strengthens and encourages those who follow Him in labor for the temporal and spiritual good of men. As an artist aiming to copy a perfect picture — the excellence of the model elevates his aim at the same time that it inspires his endeavors. And if the patron of the artist bestows his highest reward for the best exertion of the disciple, then, whatsoever degree of perfection he may attain, while he will be humbled by comparing his work with that of the master, yet his labor will be happy in its

cause their standard in Christ Jesus is always above them. Some churches have been anchored back in the shadows of the dark ages by creeds written in past periods. And even in the present age there were those in the enlightened council which assembled in Boston, in June, 1865, who desired to repudiate the principle of John Robinson, that knowledge of Holy Scripture is progressive.

progress and happy in its completion. So the Christian has hope and favor by the way; and while he is humbled by a sense of his imperfection, yet he knows that "his labors for conformity to the image of Christ are not in vain in the Lord."

§ 30.—*The truth being given in the life and precept of Christ, the second necessary thing is the work of the Spirit.*

A perfect rule of duty may be given, but to know the truth is not to love it, nor to do it. Approbation of the law does not always produce obedience to the law, nor love to the law-giver. Knowledge increases guilt, if the truth be not obeyed: hence the most intelligent men are sometimes the most base and selfish.

Man is a being of moral as well as of intellectual powers. He not only has intelligence to know the truth, but he has conscience and affections; and it is the life and impulse of these that give the truth power with the will. Men may, by an effort of intellect, enlighten each other. They may change each others opinions in regard to the truth of the Christian religion.

But in all merely intellectual changes, the heart or disposition remains the same. Correct opinions are in order to correct morals, but a man's opinions may be right, while his heart and life are wrong. Colton wrote more moral precepts than any man of his time, and violated them all. We can put truth into the mind of our fellow-man no farther than the understanding. We can not reach the moral nature by light alone. When one man changes the opinions of another on moral subjects, something is accomplished; but to give a disposition to love and obey truth is a different thing. The Holy Spirit alone sinks the truth through the intelligence into the conscience and the affections.

Truth is light, but it is not life. Alone it is like the sun in winter—it shines but to enlighten a dead, cold earth. With the Spirit, it is like the sun in summer—it shines with *life in its light*, vivifying nature and producing blade, flower and fruitage. So the light of divine truth shines in the darkness of the natural mind, and the darkness appreciates it not, until by the Spirit it becomes "spirit and life" to the soul. "In him was LIFE, and that life was the *light* of men." Christ, as the sun of righteousness, shines into believing hearts with *life* in His *light*.

§ 31.—*Rationale of the Spirit's operation in connection with the truth.*

Truth never gives life to the heart and conscience so that they are empowered to govern the will, unless there be a sense of God in it. This fact is verified in all history, as well as in the experience of individual men. The sages of antiquity perceived and announced many moral truths of the highest value,—some of them synonymous with those of the New Testament. But what care men for moral truth when it is uttered only by one whom they esteem as a fellow-mortal equal with themselves—one who has no authority to prescribe duty or to command obedience? Of what avail, in a moral estimate, was the wisdom of Plato, or the morals of Socrates, Seneca, or Tully! The moral precepts of Seneca were given to the Romans at the same time with those of Christ; in an age when the highest intelligence co-existed in the empire with the greatest profligacy. Seneca's morals had no more influence upon the character of those who received and believed them than they had upon the statues in the Pantheon. Seneca himself was accused of profligacy; and he was both the instructor and victim of the worst of the Romans. The people believed his teachings and grew worse, while those who believed the teachings of the gospel in the same age grew better. The cause of this difference is the vital point. All experience teaches that truth, separate from a sense of the authority of God, does not become life in man's moral nature. It has no efficacy to quicken the conscience or to purify the heart. There is no moral efficacy even in inspired truth, unless the soul recognizes in it the will and heart of God in regard to man. The words of Jesus had not the same efficacy before the advent of the Spirit as afterwards. Jesus taught, as we have noticed, why this was so. The God-sense was not connected with His teaching in the mind of others until after His resurrection and the advent of the Spirit; but when the Holy Ghost came, "he convinced men of sin, righteousness, and judgment," because He attached the authority and will of God to the life and teaching of Jesus. While they viewed Christ as a man like themselves they felt less sense of obligation; but when God became connected with His mission, by the miraculous resurrection, and by the advent of the Spirit, then the gospel which He had proclaimed became, to every one that believed, the hope of salvation, and the rule of duty and of judgment.

We are anxious that the reader should apprehend this point in the discussion. But we may not repeat further what we have written in other connections. We re-affirm the principle that God has so constituted the soul that conscience will enforce no moral duty unless it sees God in it. *The conscience is made to respond to the voice of God, as moral Ruler, and it will answer to no other.* A false faith may pervert the conscience to enforce a false rule, because faith has the same effect upon our moral powers as knowledge: but this only proves that a sense of God by faith is the natural life of the conscience, and that there is no other power to enforce truth but conscience. It proves also that revealed truth, or truth that carries the authority of God with it, is an absolute necessity in order to the regeneration of men. Truth, by human authority alone, can not accomplish the end. Hence the advent of the Spirit was the great promise, because it gave the God-sense to Christ's life and teaching. The apostles did not move from their place until it descended upon them: then, illumined and empowered, they went forth (Eph. iii, 9) "to make all men see what is the fellowship of the mystery, which from the beginning of the world hath been hid in God, who created all things by Jesus Christ."

§ 32.—*The preceding views illustrated by experience.*

The preceding views will be recognized as verified in the experience of most persons. A man may hear the truth without impression at one time, and yet, at another time, by *the same truth*, presented, it may be, in a more feeble manner, he will be made conscious that he is a sinner in the sight of God. In such cases, if he will examine his exercises, he will see that it is the sense of God's authority in connection with truth, which gives it its efficacy. It is the same mind and the same truth, and it may be the same instrumentality; but in one case it produces no effect, except an intellectual impression, in the other it produces prayer, penitence, and reformation of life. Experience thus verifies the testimony of the Bible, that the spiritual sense is necessary to the efficacy of Divine truth.

§ 33.—*The sum of preceding deductions.*

The conscience being quickened by the truth through the Spirit, the soul is awakened; the heart being affected by the love of Christ, as His life and death are exhibited by the Spirit, the soul is converted; and the moral and emotional nature thus vitalized, act upon the will, and produce obedience by influencing it into harmony with the will of Christ. When conscience and the heart thus unite their power, they determine the will potentially. Conscience enforces the rule of righteousness as duty to God—the heart induces obedience by love to the person whose will is obeyed. Hence, *as the rule of righteousness and the personal will of Christ are one*, the Redeemer becomes "the way, the truth, and the life to every one that believeth."

This revelation of the rule of life by the personal example and will of Christ is necessary to satisfy the wants, as well as to meet the nature of the soul; *obedience to an abstract law, without the recognition of a personal will in that law*, can never satisfy the heart. It is absurd to talk, as the skeptics do, of love and obedience to the laws of nature, or to anything impersonal.* Affectionate obedience, as we have noticed, can be exercised only towards a *personal* being who has voluntarily, and in view of our wants, exercised himself in goodness towards us. The man who talks about a "religion of nature" for man, has surely not studied the necessities of man's moral nature. There can be no affectionate obedience to a superior being, except in view of the character and action of that being as personally related to us. As man is made, the motive to obedience must be an apprehension of the character and qualities of the law-giver. Hence the Spirit comes to us in the name of Christ, exhibiting the Father in the person of the Son, and exhibiting His law and His love together as prerogative and attribute of His person. Thus the soul finds *motive in Christ* for affectionate obedience to Him as Lord and Saviour. Oh, the length, and the breadth, and the depth, and the height of that Divine wisdom which has given the rule of duty in connection with a revelation of love, and in the one person of Christ; so

* See note on Parker, Emerson, and Transcendentalism in Appendix.

that the conscience and affections unite in producing love to the Law-giver!

§ 34.—*The union of the Word and Spirit necessary in the process of conviction and sanctification.*

In one sense truth gives direction without moral impulse, and the Spirit gives moral impulse without direction. There are multitudes who sometimes see the light and desire to obey, but "are not able." To use a phraseology common with such, "they have no heart." On the contrary, in times of special religious interest in any community, many apparently become willing to obey who have no right apprehension of the example of Christ as the rule of duty. The truth in regard to the evil of sin in the sight of God is *felt* by them. The conscience awakes, the man in a sense repents, but he is like a blind man running from the flames,—he runs to stumble, and to stop he knows not where. The heart of the man dispossessed of evil demons[*] was swept and garnished,—he had in one sense repented from sin, but his mind, although "swept and garnished," remained unoccupied. He had

[*] Matt. xii, 44.

not enthroned Christ as Lord and Saviour; hence the evil returned with greater power. It is only when faith connects the precept with the person of Christ — His law with His love — that both direction and impulse are given to the will.

There is often, likewise, in the minds of sincere persons, an imperfect apprehension of truth. The character of Christ may be perceived truly in one regard, and imperfectly in another. The devotee may have faith in a dying Christ, but little apprehension of the living Christ as the rule of life; this will stir his emotions, and produce love to God without labor for men. The Reformer may have faith in the life of Christ; this will move to good works, but such works do not flow from that love which purifies the heart. The Sectarian may believe in a creed rather than in Christ; this will make him compass sea and land to make proselytes to a sect rather than to the Saviour. Hence faith in the living example and dying love of Christ are both necessary. A living conscience and heart are the only true motive-powers in the service of God. These are awakened by a sense of God in truth, and by Christ's suffering in the flesh for us. Good works for the temporal and spiritual good of man are the only true life,—these are produced by conformity of the human will by love to the will of Christ. Thus faith in Christ's life and death combined gives both impulse and direction to the religious life. And unless our motives to action are thus drawn from Christ, the impulse and end of our life must be in ourselves,—our works will be "dead works," and assimilation to the Divine image can not be the result of our activity.

§ 35.—*The preceding views accord with the relations of the Word and Spirit, as they exist in both the finite and the Infinite mind.*

In the human mind, and in the Divine mind, as presented in preceding pages, the Word, or Logos, is the intelligence — the conceived and uttered thought or outbirth of the soul. The Spirit is back of the Word. It knows* the Word, and uses it to reveal its own character to other minds, *so far as it designs its personal character and will to be known.* It is thus in the process

---

* 1 Cor. ii, 11,—"For what man knoweth the things of a man, save the spirit of man which is in him? even so the things of God knoweth no man, but the Spirit of God."

of human redemption from ignorance and sin: the operation of the Divine mind, and the relation and manifestation of Word and Spirit, are revealed as acting in accordance with this constitutional method of mental development. The Spirit uses the Word—takes of its manifestation—and thus through the Word, and by the Word, as Messiah or Mediator, reveals God, and redeems those who believe. Men are thus "sanctified by the Spirit through the Truth," as it was lived, spoken, and suffered by the Son of God.

§ 36.—*The preceding views confirmed by the teaching of the Scriptures.*

It will not be necessary to recite in this section all the various passages in which the Word and Spirit are spoken of in their related efficacy. In Scripture the Word is "the sword of the Spirit." Men are said to be "sanctified by the truth through the Spirit." The apostles announce the relation frequently and clearly; showing that in their own minds the subject was distinctly apprehended. Peter, in exhorting believers to the exercise of Christian love, says (1 Peter i, 22),

"Seeing ye have purified your souls *in obeying the truth through the* SPIRIT unto unfeigned love of the brethren, see that ye love one another with a pure heart fervently." This is the import of the whole matter,—by the Word and Spirit affectionate obedience is produced toward God, and fraternal love toward men.

So the same general view, that truth in the mind is a pre-requisite to the permanent and perfect work of the Spirit, is set forth by the Saviour Himself in the parable of the sower. Matt. xiii,—" He that heareth the word and *comprehendeth it not*, straightway the evil one cometh and catcheth away that which was sown in his heart. But he that receiveth seed into good ground is he that heareth the word, and *understandeth it;* which also beareth fruit, and bringeth forth, some an hundredfold, some sixty, some thirty."

A reception of the revealed word into an appreciative mind is necessary in order to the fruit of obedience. All fanaticism grows out of a disseverance of the Spirit and the revealed Word. All erring enthusiasts are persuaded that the Spirit teaches them separate from, or beyond, what is written. They do not "understand" that the Spirit does not come to reveal new truth, but to use the truth which Christ has already revealed. Men can be purified only by "obeying the truth through the Spirit." The man who understands the truth and does not obey is a sinner. The man who professes to be influenced by the Spirit, while he does not obey Christ by a life of labor for human good, is an enthusiast.* But if we "abide in Christ" by *faith*, "and his word abide in us" by *understanding*, we shall then have both the impulse of the Spirit and the guidance of the Word. Prayer will be answered; and we "shall neither be barren nor unfruitful in the knowledge of our Lord and Saviour Jesus Christ."

* See Appendix E,—CAUSE OF FANATICISM

CHAPTER VI.

THE WORK OF CHRIST BY THE DIVINE SPIRIT IN THE MINDS OF BELIEVERS.

"*I will not leave you comfortless: I will come unto you.*"* The promise of Christ in this language and in other phraseology, to come again after His ascension to the Father, is often spoken of by the sacred writers. There are three events to which the promise in some of its phrases is applicable. The first, and the most important in its spiritual significance, is the coming of Christ, by the Holy Spirit, to guide, comfort, and sanctify believers, and to convince the world of sin, righteousness, and judgment. To His disciples He said, "I will not leave you comfortless: I will come unto you." This was His coming in the Comforter. John xiv, 19,— "The world seeth me no more; but ye shall

---

* John xiv, 18.

see me; because I live, ye shall live also." In Him was life, and that life would be light and love in them. They would be conscious of His indwelling presence, when He should reveal Himself to them as He did not to the world. This was His first coming. He came again *by His providence*, to destroy the city and the temple, and with these the ritual dispensation of Moses. The gospel being engrafted upon the Old Dispensation, it was fit, in the order of progress, that the imperfect should pass away, so that the perfect might supervene.* He will come again *in person*, at the end of the Christian Dispensation, to judge mankind, to destroy the wicked and the world together,† and to inaugurate "the new heavens and the new earth, in which shall dwell the righteous," who possess eternal life by their union with Him.

But Christ's coming *by His Spirit* is the great event of the New Dispensation. The apostles themselves did not apprehend, until after the fulfillment of the promise, the plenitude and the

---

* Heb. xii, 27, — " Signifieth the removing of those things that are shaken, as of things that are made, that those things which cannot be shaken may remain."

2 Pet. iii.

power of the blessing which the words indicated.*

§ 37. — *The twofold office-work of the Spirit.*

The work of the Spirit is twofold, in the Church, and in the world,— *in* the minds of those who are reconciled to God, and *with* the minds of the disobedient.

Whether the Holy Spirit ever influences the disobedient, unless it be dispensed through the Church — through the minds of believers, as a medium, is a question that should receive thoughtful consideration. It is one of great practical importance; and, believing that the Divine procedure ordinarily is, that the Spirit is dispensed to believing and obedient minds, and through these to the unregenerate, we will speak of His work in this order.

"The promise of the Father" was given first to the disciples. To them the Spirit came, in power, on the day of Pentecost. They immediately began their mission, and preached Christ crucified as Lord and Saviour. The Divine Spirit

---

* See Appendix,— PRIMITIVE VIEWS IN REGARD TO CHRIST'S SECOND ADVENT.

and Divine providence co-operated with their effort. Men were "pricked in their hearts," and inquired what they should do. They were instructed to believe on the Lord Jesus Christ; and thus believing with their heart, they were baptized and added to the churches.

The necessity of the Spirit's work, and His separate office with the obedient and disobedient mind, are stated with great distinctness by the Saviour in His last conversation with the disciples. We will quote the whole passage in this place, in order that we may mark the order and the significance of the words. The instruction which they contain will form for the most part the subject matter of succeeding pages.

John xvi, 7–16,—"I tell you the truth; it is expedient for you that I go away: for if I go not away, the Comforter will not come unto you; but if I depart, I will send him unto you.

" And when he is come, he will convince the world of sin, of righteousness, and of judgment:

" Of sin, because they believe not on me;

" Of righteousness, because I go to the Father, and ye see me no more:

" And of judgment, because the Prince of this world is judged.

"I have yet many things to say unto you, but ye can not bear them now. Howbeit when he, the Spirit of Truth, is come, he will lead you unto all truth: for he shall not speak of himself; but whatsoever things he shall hear, that shall he speak: and he will show you things to come.

"He shall glorify me; for he shall receive of mine, and shall show it unto you.

"All things that the Father hath are mine: therefore said I, that he shall take of mine, and shall show it unto you.

"A little while, and ye shall not see me: and again, a little while, and ye shall see me, because I go to the Father."

It is not necessary in this connection to speak of the miraculous manifestations of the Spirit in the apostolic age. The foregoing passage, which specifies the work of the promised Comforter, does not include these. Miracles were for a sign. They were the divine credentials confirming the mission of those who established the New Dispensation. As such, they were necessary, in view of the state of the human mind, in the beginning of all the dispensations. The burden of the promise in the New Testament is, *con-*

viction of sin TO THE WORLD, *and sanctification* TO BELIEVERS, *through the truth of Christ, empowered by the Holy Ghost.* The spiritual import of the subject is of the highest moment. It speaks of the connection where the Divine unites itself with the human, in working out the salvation of the soul. We will consider it in the several aspects presented in the foregoing words of Christ, and endeavor to apprehend distinctly the process of the Spirit, working by the Truth *in* the believing, and *upon* the unbelieving, mind. First, in the believing mind.

§ 38.— *The experimental import of the statement that the Spirit shall not speak of Himself.*

We have referred to this statement in preceding pages,— let us now endeavor to gain an appreciation of the experimental meaning of the words, " *The Spirit shall not speak of Himself.*"

When the soul is influenced by the Divine Messenger, the believer is not led to think of the Spirit itself, nor to utter praise in view of the person and work of the Spirit; but the person and work of Christ is brought before the mind. The Comforter takes of the things that belong to Jesus, and shows them to the soul. The self-denial of the Redeemer, the lowliness and loveliness of His character, His mercy to the sinful, His suffering as a ransom — some view of His character or work, as it relates to the human soul, is presented; "and while the Christian muses the fire burns." A glow of devotion is awakened in his emotions that purifies and empowers. 2 Cor. iii, 18, — He "sees as in a glass the glory of God, and is changed into the same image from glory to glory, *even as by the Spirit of the Lord.*"

> There is an affluence supplied
> By faith in Christ the crucified,
>   Through all the being rife;
> It is the power that makes us whole—
> A saving unction in the soul—
>   *It is the Spirit's life.*

The specialty of the statement ought to be particularly noted. It is not in accordance with the aim and effect of ordinary spiritual intercourse. The impression of one spirit upon another usually attracts the attention of the one addressed to the personality of the one which communicates the thought. But the Spirit of God does not exhibit Himself, but He exhibits the personality of Christ to the mind. *He awakens the soul to introduce the Saviour.* The personality which the soul sees is that of Jesus; and the truth which the Spirit uses is limited and bounded by the Redeemer's work. The believer experiences the fulfillment of the promise, "He shall take of the things that belong to me and show them unto you."

§ 39.—*By exhibiting Christ the Spirit likewise exhibits the Father to the soul.*

The Scriptures teach, as we have seen, that all the attributes of the Father that are *knowable* by man are revealed in the Son. The Son, or Word, is the "outshining of the Father's glory, and the perfect image of His personality. Thus the Father in Christ, and Christ by the Spirit, is revealed to the obedient mind. "All things that the Father hath are mine: therefore said I, he [the Spirit] shall take of mine, and show it unto you."

It was promised to the apostles that the Spirit should form a conscious spiritual union between their souls and Christ, and through Christ with the Father. John xiv, 20, 23,—"At that day ye shall know that I am in the Father, and ye in me, and I in you." "If a man love me he will keep my commandments: and my Father will love him, and WE [Father and Son] will come and make our abode with him." So in 1 John ii, 14,—"Ye have an unction from the Holy One, and ye know all things, and if that which ye have heard from the beginning remain in you, ye shall continue in the Son and in the Father."

"I in them and thou in me; that they may be made perfect in one." These mystic words are true in the consciousness of believers; and the form of this spiritual union is verified in the nature of mind. By the Holy Spirit the Father is in Christ, and Christ in believers: one consciousness of life and love flowing from the one God through all individual holy minds in the universe. "Glory be to the Father, and to the Son, and to the Holy Ghost; as it was in the beginning — is now, and ever shall be — world without end."

How clear, yet how profound and beneficent, is the Divine manifestation! Believers are made "partakers of the Divine nature." The nature of the Father through the Son is made known unto them — and (to repeat an illustration) as the rays of light which pass through a colored medium take the hues of the medium through which they come, so the Spirit of God, coming to us through Christ incarnate, is baptized in the humanities of His person, and hence becomes the dispenser of the Divine mercy, as that mercy was revealed in the flesh. So that (Rom. viii, 3, 4), "What the law could not do, in that it was weak through the flesh [had no sympathetic power to touch the emotional nature], God sending his own Son in the likeness of sinful flesh, and for sin, condemned sin in the flesh: that the righteousness of the law [which requires love but can not produce it] might be fulfilled in us, who walk not after the flesh, but the Spirit."

§ 40.—*The Spirit witnesses to the truth of Divine revelation.*

"He that believeth on the Son of God hath the witness in himself" (1 John v, 10) that the record which God has given of His Son is true. The form of this testimony is obvious. The mental exercises, — the hopes, fears, interests, states of mind, which those possessed who believed the truth in the age of the apostles, are given in the New Testament. These were produced by belief of the truth as then revealed. By the Holy Spirit the same truth begets the same state of mind in believers now that is promised in the record, and that was possessed by believers of the age when it was spoken. The Christian *knows* therefore that it is *the same Spirit* and *the same truth* that existed in the days of the apostles, because the same effects are produced in him, by the same cause, which were produced in them. The promise of light, comfort, strength, by the Spirit is fulfilled; and he can no more doubt the truth of the Christian religion, than he could doubt the word of a traveler, who told him of a spring by the wayside after he had himself found it as described, and tasted the qualities of the water, which refreshed and strengthened him, as it had others.

This is the assurance of Paul, when he says, "The Holy Ghost also is witness for us."* He predicated his statement, as the passage shows, upon the promise given in the Old Testament,

* Heb. x, 15.

that in the time of Christ the "law should be written in the heart." This was fulfilled in him by the Spirit, and therefore he knew, by the highest of all evidence, that both the Old Testament promises and the New Testament experience were from God. The one was the counterpart of the other.

Many persons, not apprehending the nature of the infallible evidence for spiritual religion, ask Why does not God give us now the same miraculous testimony to the truth of revelation that He gave to His ancient people? We have better testimony than this:—The presence of Christ by His Spirit is better evidence than was His presence by the pillar of cloud and fire. The one was better adapted to the age of infancy and discipline—the other is adapted to the age of manhood and reason. In the one Christ was present to the sense—in the other He is present to the soul. The Shekinah which shone through the veil of Moses, now shines unveiled into the hearts of believers, giving them the "light of the knowledge of God in the face of Christ Jesus.'

The conscious testimony of the Holy Spirit is

the only satisfactory evidence of faith in Christ.* The external evidence of the truth of Christianity may convince the intelligence of some men that the system has historical validity. The use of such evidence is proper in its place; and in the hands of those who understand its place and its comparative value it may be used with profit to others. But some have written on the evidences of Christianity that knew nothing themselves of the higher testimony. And many have believed the history of "God manifest in the flesh," who never possessed the inward testimony produced by the "faith which works by love and purifies the heart."† Such men may discuss, with much learning and intellectual acumen, the dogma of theological systems: but it is written (1 Cor. xii, 3), and will be true for ever, that "no man can say Jesus is the Christ but by the Holy Ghost."

---

* See Appendix G,— BISHOP TAYLOR'S TESTIMONY.

† The Spirit was not promised to testify of the canon of the Old Testament, or the Hagiography, or histories of Old Testament times. It testifies of the Old Testament system as introductory, and hence immature both in precept and example. Its promised "conviction of sin" is in view of Christ, and it "takes of the things that belong to Christ and shows them to the believer," and to the believer only.

This view of the place and comparative value of miraculous and spiritual testimony is recognized by the Saviour. Before the advent of the Spirit, and while Jesus was yet with them, He urged His disciples, and likewise the Jews, to believe that the Father was in Him, and He in the Father, for the works' sake which He did. Before the day of Pentecost, miracles were the best evidence that men had of the divinity of Christ. And down to this day, with unregenerate minds, and Christians in the Old Testament or John Baptist state, miracles are still the best testimony which such possess. But at the same time that Christ appealed to His miracles as evidence of His commission from Heaven, He promised to His disciples more satisfactory testimony — a testimony which the world did not and could not receive. John xiv, 11—26,—"He that loveth me shall be loved of my Father, and I will love him, and will manifest myself to him." "*At that day ye shall* KNOW *that I am in the Father, and ye in me, and I in you.*"

§ 41. — *The nature of the Spirit's witness.*

The visitations of the Spirit are with the inner life of the soul. They beget a sense of sonship in the believing mind. The renewed man is willing to obey and be treated as a servant, but he is received and endowed with the spirit and privileges of a son. In regeneration the mind passes, as the Church has done, through the legal into the spiritual dispensation. All the demands of conscience are obeyed better than before, but the impulse to will and to do is born in the heart. The Old Testament servant becomes a New Testament son. "Our Father" is the proper designation of God under the new dispensation. But it is a designation specially appropriate to those in whose minds the law of love is fulfilled. "They that are *led by the Spirit of God*, they are the sons of God." Hence Paul, in speaking of the obedience he once offered, and that which he then enjoyed, says (Rom. viii, 15, 16), "For we have not received the spirit of bondage again to fear; but we have received the Spirit of adoption, whereby we cry, Abba, Father,— the *Spirit itself* bearing witness with our spirit, that we are the sons of God."

Of this condition of sonship, as of all other Christian graces and glories, Jesus Christ Himself is the example and the type. From Him, by the Spirit, believers receive into their hearts the Christian virtues — "grace for grace." Each lineament of His character is impressed upon them in proportion to their faith. So that the devout, tender, and submissive spirit manifested by Christ toward the Father, is reproduced in believers "by the Spirit of Christ which dwelleth in them." Gal. iv, 6, — "For God hath sent forth the Spirit of his Son into their hearts, crying, Abba, Father."

§ 42.— *The influence of the Spirit upon the faculties of the mind separately considered.*

The Spirit of Christ does not work in contravention of the normal exercise of the mental powers. On the contrary, it works in harmony with all the laws of mind. Its influence is to exhilarate and exercise the mental faculties joyfully and energetically. The things which Christ had spoken were brought to the memory of the disciples, but this was done evidently according to the law of suggestion. The different evangelists in communicating the same truth connect it sometimes with one incident, and sometimes with another; each recording the event as suggested by the circumstance which most affected him, and each presenting it in language in keeping with his natural temperament, and with the degree of his mental culture.* One evangelist associates events topically, another logically, and another spiritually; but still in all the memory furnishes the same truth, characterized by the diverse advantages and mental peculiarities of the writers.

A spiritual mind is one awakened to life and interest in spiritual things. To the Christian preacher especially, this *heart-interest* in the gospel is an essential qualification. The affections, awakened by faith, will start the law of suggestion, and thus give parallel texts to the memory, and freshness of illustration to impress

---

* When Bible orators speak of the excellence of Revelation, as consisting in the wonderful sublimity of language and wonderful excellence of precept found in the Old and New Testament. they no doubt ought to be commended for their well-meant efforts. But it is certain that literary style in any other sense than as a specimen of the *usus loquendi* of the age, was not designed to be an evidence of inspiration. If literary excellence was the criterion of judgment, it would be difficult for well-informed Christians to undertake the proof of Divine inspiration. Even if the precepts of the Bible were its chief excellence the evidence would be different from what it really is. The example and precepts of Christ are perfect and ultimate,

the thought. Every true minister understands and appreciates this fact, and every audience, *without knowing why*, feels it. As a man pleading for his child will find words, and be impressive in tone and gesture, so a believing mind will be aided, and will communicate of its *animus* to those who hear.

Earnestnes, love, and other qualities of thought which characterize true gospel services, are mere affectations in some pulpits. Men are conscious of what their profession requires, and perhaps from a laudable but heartless sense of propriety assume the adapted manner. But such preachers do not " speak as of the ability that God giveth, that God in all things may be glorified."† They speak as of themselves; and the false fire upon

---

' Thou shalt love God with all thy heart and all thy might, and thy neighbor as thyself." There can be nothing purer nor higher than this. Any thing else would be wrong. If God were to give another religion it would necessarily be a worse one, because it could not be better. But *the* POWER *of the gospel is its glory.* The *strength* imparted by the Spirit through the conscience and the heart to obey Christ as a personal Saviour, is its vital excellence. The disposition to do the good that we know is the great want of the soul. *This want is supplied by faith in Christ.* This precept enlightens. THE SPIRIT GIVES LIFE.

† 1 Pet. iv, 11.

the altar is a proper emblem of their service. "Out of the abundance of the heart the mouth speaketh;" and when a true minister has carefully and prayerfully prepared a discourse, forgetting himself and shaping it under the motive to do good, if the manuscript be not so closed as to prevent it, he will get from the impulse within him aids and suggestions which will greatly add to the impression of his teaching.*

It may be that the mind that is naturally impulsive and sanguine, as it is, in itself, more liable to mistakes, is likewise, from its temperament, more susceptible of aid than others. Such were the minds of Peter, Luther, Whitfield and Finney. There are some men who are so careful lest they should do evil that they never do much good — so careful to avoid error that they fail to exhibit truth. Some prepare a sermon with the selfish thought in their minds, *What effect will this presentation have upon* ME *in the estimation of the audience?* Some close a manuscript in such form that there is no place for the Holy Spirit to put in a suggestion. Hence a fervent, sincere, believing mind will most fre-

* See on this general subject the excellent book of W. Arthur, M.A., entitled "*The Tongue of Fire.*"

quently be aided; and even the blunders to which it is liable will often be overruled for good,— for good, both to humble the speaker and to benefit the hearer. It is difficult, however, to discriminate between the line of selfish caution and sinful presumption. God alone, not man, is judge.

The promise to the apostles that they would be aided without forethought related only to *exigencies*, and ought not to be claimed for the formal, routine preaching of our age. But, in every age, spiritual aid to prepare and to speak is, without doubt, granted to all evangelists who have a true faith, and who seek to accomplish the end for which the Holy Spirit gives strength to the soul: — the great end of all Christian effort,— to glorify God by doing good to men.

But while the Spirit thus operates in accordance with the conformation of the mind, there are exceptional cases where abnormal conformation interferes with symmetrical religious development. There are minds in which certain powers or susceptibilities are dwarfed or perverted. The susceptibility of hope, for instance, may be overactive or it may be almost wanting. In such cases, without a miracle, a full and perfect development of religious life is not possible. A phlegmatic temperament will not be likely to express itself in sanguine appeals. Grace may compensate for want in one direction by strength in another, but it will not equalize the development. But notwithstanding these diversities, there are two qualities, or powers, to which faith will always give vitality and position. In all cases, however defective may be some of the intellectual powers, the conscience will be enthroned and the affections will receive new life; and these moral powers, raised by faith to headship in the soul,* will determine the strength of the motive,† and give impulse to the will. Righteousness and the love of God will be in the ascendant. There will be different phases of manifestation; and fruits will be matured in different degrees of abundance, and of different qualities —still, in the life of every true Christian, conscience and love will rule; and the fruits of the Spirit, borne on all the branches united to Christ, will be "love, joy, peace, long-suffering, gentle-

---

* See Chalmers' Bridgewater Treatise on the Supremacy of Conscience.

† The power of motive-truth depends upon the state of mind upon which it operates.

ness, goodness, faith, meekness, temperance." These the soul will taste in its own susceptibility, and will thus be made to partake of the fruit of the " Tree of Life, which groweth in the midst of the Paradise of God."

§ 43.—*The duty of prayer annexed to the doctrine of the Spirit.*

The gift of the Spirit of Truth, as we have noticed, is the promise of the Father — the promise of Christ — the great promise of the New Testament Dispensation. The believer is not only invited to ask for this offered blessing, but he is apparently entreated by the Author of all Mercies to seek for that spiritual presence of Christ which is, in itself, *an answer to all prayer.* "Seek, and ye shall find;" "Ask, and it shall be given unto you." We are taught that the Divine Father is more willing to give the Holy Spirit to His children who ask Him than earthly parents are to give good gifts to their offspring. And annexed to this promise there is the assurance that the blessing granted shall not be such as to mock the suppliant; but that it will be a satisfactory supply of his spiritual wants. "If a child ask bread, will a parent give him a stone?" something that will mock, but not satisfy his want? Even so, the Father in Heaven will grant a *satisfying supply for the spiritual wants* of those who ask Him.

Such is the plentitude of the promise to the children of God. And they are encouraged to seek spiritual blessings, not only for themselves, but in answer to their *persevering* supplication, blessings are promised TO THEM, *for others*, and they are constituted the mediums through which spiritual mercies are communicated to those who have not tasted of the bread of life,* and for whom they make supplication.

§ 44.—*The condition upon which he influence of the Holy Spirit is granted.*

It is not every form o prayer. that is answered by a blessing. It is (James v, 16) "The effectual fervent prayer of the righteous man that availeth much." Some things are required in the character of the suppliant, and some things in the quality of the prayer. The sum of these requirements, as to character, is tha the sup-

---

* See Luke xi, 5—13.

pliant should live up to his knowledge of duty. We must not refuse to use the light and strength which we possess while we pray for more light and aid from above.

The golden rule is a deduction of the reason, as well as a precept of revelation.* We know by experience what we desire others should or should not do to us, hence we know what we ought to do to them. In Matthew vii, 11, 12, the Saviour's promise of the Spirit is immediately conjoined with this rule of righteousness. He says, " If ye, being evil, know how to give good gifts unto your children, how much more shall your Father which is in Heaven give good gifts to them that ask him?" " *Therefore*, all things whatsoever ye would that men should do unto you, do ye even so unto them." The Christian, therefore, who labors to practice this rule, comes acceptably to the Father for the aid of the promised Spirit.

The Apostle Paul gives the same truth and the same connection in another form of words (Phil. iii, 14, 15),—" I press toward the mark for the prize of the high calling of God in Christ

---

* Confucius announced this rule in words the import of which is precisely the same as that taught in the language of Jesus.

Jesus. Let us, therefore, as many as be perfect, be thus minded: and if in any thing ye be otherwise minded, God will reveal even this unto you." That is, if in the discharge of Christian duty you use all the strength at present granted, God will aid you in regard to other things which you may desire. And this promise of increase, when the measure of ability is complied with, relates not only to duty but to doctrine. John vii, 17,—" If any man will do his will, he shall know of the doctrine whether it be of God."

The Apostle John gives the specific sense (1 John iii, 21, 22),—" Beloved, if our heart condemn us not, then have we confidence toward God. *And whatsoever we ask we receive of him*, BECAUSE WE KEEP HIS COMMANDMENTS, AND DO THOSE THINGS WHICH ARE PLEASING IN HIS SIGHT." That is, in order to receive an answer to prayer for promised blessings, we must be living, so far as we have ability, in the discharge of all duties that we know are pleasing to God. It is mockery to pray, as some do, for guidance and strength, while they are not obedient so far as they have knowledge and ability. It is the same thing as refusing to use the ability granted us, while yet we ask for more.

If the Scriptures make any thing plain, it is that *good works, as of the ability that God giveth, are required in order that prayer may be answered.* In the parable of Jesus, he who had the one talent committed to him was a servant who professed to fear and obey his master. He was not one of the rebellious citizens who hated their Lord and opposed His government. And while thus refusing to exercise his ability in the use of the talent committed to him, he not only failed of a present blessing by an increase of his talent arising from the use of it, but he secured for himself merited penalty. His soul was not slain as the rebellious citizen, but it was darkened, and possessed with regretful exercises.*

---

* See Luke xix, 11-27.—A penalty is affixed to the non-use of our faculties and abilities, both in nature and grace. The man who, like the Fakir in India, refuses to use his arm, will lose ability to use it. The man who refuses to use his moral faculties in the service of God, will lose moral strength in the faculty which is not exercised. All our faculties gain strength by exercise, and lose strength by non-use. The unprofitable servant in the parable professed to know the character, and to fear the frown, of his master. He knew his master had power to do as he pleased, and did not need his service; and seeing he was *so sovereign*, he did not himself know what to do with the talent intrusted to him. So he kept it very care-

Suppose that God should grant the Holy Spirit in answer to prayer, without the condition that the servant should use the ability already possessed; the answer would, in such case, mislead the suppliant and tend to licentiousness. The fact that God had given peace and love where there was pride and prejudice and disobedience (if such a thing were possible — which it is not), would lead the suppliant to believe that God was pleased with him while he possessed a wrong state of heart, and was not letting the light he already possessed shine, according to the commandment. Thus man would be deceived and injured, and God would be dishonored. The best Christians sometimes feel the weakness

fully (had very careful habits, and did not abuse his moral powers in any way), and returned it in good condition to him who gave it. Such a professed servant of Christ, we are taught, will hereafter be cast out into moral darkness, where he will be filled with compunction in view of his indolence and folly. The enemies of Christ who refuse to have Him reign over them, are brought out and slain before Him. The unprofitable servant suffers loss, exclusion, and remorse. The rebels are destroyed.

Let unprofitable servants, whose names are legion, notice the specific difference between the *reward* of the profitable servant, the *doom* of the unprofitable, and the *destruction* of the rebellious citizen.

of their strength and of their faith, but they know the will of God and can obey with a prayerful, dependent, and persevering spirit; and while doing the work of a servant, if they do it for Christ's sake, God will recognize them as sons. When comparing themselves with Christ, all Christians will see imperfection in their obedience — but they will be conscious of an obedient spirit, and trust in Christ's mercy, and this is the true Christian consciousness in light or darkness.

To the young convert whose heart is purified, and whose knowledge is yet limited, the privilege of the newly born may be given. The Good Shepherd may take the lamb in His arms, and bear it for a time in His bosom; but He will set it down in order that it may gain strength by exercise. So the young Christian must learn to talk, and walk, and work. He may lean on Christ's strength, but he must exercise his faculties in active service; and refusing to do this he will fail in fruitfulness, and fail of the favor of God in answer to prayer.

The requirement of reason and of Scripture, in regard to the instructed Christian in order to communion with God, is that he should live so that his conscience does not condemn him for neglecting known duty. 1 John iii, 19-22,— "Hereby we know that we are of the truth, and shall assure our hearts before him. For if our conscience condemn us, God is greater than our conscience, and knoweth all things. Beloved, if our conscience condemn us not, then have we confidence toward God. *And whatsoever we ask, we receive of him*, BECAUSE WE KEEP HIS COMMANDMENTS, AND DO THE THINGS THAT ARE PLEASING IN HIS SIGHT." This is explicit. No one but the formal worshiper can fail to understand.

§ 45. — *Availing prayer is offered to God in the name of Christ.*

The Redeemer, in His last words with His disciples, speaking of His departure from them, and the new views which would be attained, and the new duties which would supervene after His ascension, says (John xvi, 23, 24), " In that day [after I shall have fully revealed the Father and ascended to his bosom] ye shall ask me nothing. Verily, verily, I say unto you, Whatsoever ye shall ask the Father *in my name*, he will give it you. Hitherto ye have asked nothing in my name: ask, and receive, that your joy may be full."

When we ask for spiritual blessings, viewing the Father's character as revealed in Christ, "the Father is glorified in the Son." This is the import of this and other parallel passages.* To ask the Father in the name of Christ, is to ask Him in the character which the work of Christ has given Him. He is thus glorified in the name, or in the character, which He has revealed in Christ. If God's character were not viewed through Christ, we would not be regarding His moral excellences and His relations to ourselves as they really exist under the New Testament dispensation. God is as good as the sacrifice of Christ reveals Him to be. To know Him, therefore, as He is, to worship in the light of His true character, we must ask in the name of Jesus; that is, adoring the Divine Being as revealed in the Mediator.

Before the crucifixion and the advent of the Spirit the disciples had made supplication in the name of Jehovah—the name by which the attributes of God were imperfectly revealed in

---

* See Philosophy of Plan of Salvation, chap. xvii.

the Old Testament dispensation; but when the Spirit led them to see the Father in Christ, then, and not till then, Christ's name was associated in all their addresses to the Supreme Being.* Heb. xiii, 20, 21,—" Now the God of peace, that brought again from the dead our Lord Jesus Christ, that great shepherd of the sheep, through the blood of the everlasting covenant, make you perfect in every good work to do his will, working in you that which is well pleasing in his sight, through Jesus Christ; to whom be glory for ever and ever. Amen."

§ 46.—*The sum of preceding sections.*

The sum of preceding thoughts on this subject is, that prayer for the blessing of the Spirit,

---

* A true faith in Christ implies both the impulse of love and the guidance of truth. Many have faith in Christ as a Saviour, who misapprehend, or are ignorant of His will in regard to duty. They pray not in submission, but for strength to do what is contrary to the will of God. They have zeal without knowledge. To hear their prayer would be to grant them strength to misdirect their efforts. Their prayer may be answered; but not in the manner they desire. But those who " *abide in Christ by faith*, and in whom *his words abide* as guidance, may ask what they will, and it shall be *done unto them*."—John xv, 7.

when we are not living up to our light, nor making an effort to do so, is mockery. Supplication for the Spirit's guidance, when we are at the same time unwilling to be made the humble, obedient, self-denying Christians which we know the Spirit would make us, is hypocrisy. But to those who receive the words of Christ and are obedient to them in heart — to such as endeavor, according to their ability, to exemplify the Spirit and follow the example of the Great Teacher, the Comforter is promised, and the promise will never fail while the truth and mercy of God endure.

And when the Comforter comes, He not only brings a blessing to the soul of the suppliant, but He endues him with a blessing for the subjects of his prayers. Not that impenitent men will be converted when the believer makes persistent supplication for them; but, if they have not sinned beyond recovery, the Divine Spirit will visit those for whom such supplication is offered, and by some fact of providence, or of revelation, such minds will be impressed and invited to consider subjects connected with their spiritual condition here and their spiritual wellbeing hereafter.

Thus the company of obedient Christians are made "partakers of the Divine nature," and become the living mediums by which the mercy of Heaven is conveyed through the earth. They are appointed "a holy priesthood, to offer up spiritual sacrifices, acceptable to God, through Jesus Christ." Under the Old Testament, the company of priests made intercession, "with sacrifice, day by day, which could not make them which did the service perfect as pertaining to the conscience." Under the new and perfect dispensation, every believer is appointed an intercessor. For them the sacrifice of Christ is always offered—" offered once for all *by the Eternal Spirit.*" Whoever believes and obeys Christ receives the Spirit; his work for the good of men will then be availing, and his prayers will be answered,—for he is constituted "a king and priest unto God, and he shall reign in the new heavens and new earth, in which dwelleth righteousness." *

* Rev. v, 10. See Appendix H,—CONNECTION BETWEEN TRUTH, PROVIDENCE, AND PRAYER.

CHAPTER VII.

THE WORK OF THE HOLY SPIRIT WITH THE MINDS OF THE IMPENITENT.

The Holy Spirit being given to believers, as in the preceding chapter, and they exercising themselves as laborers and intercessors for the sinful and the needy, then the Divine influence will follow their thought, or will otherwise reach the minds of those for whom they make supplication; and such minds will (unless unusual obstacles prevent) be led to think of God, of sin, and of duty. Wherever there is effort and prayer for the glory of God in the good of men, such supplication and effort produce effect in some direction, and upon some person or persons; usually, as we have said, upon those for whom the supplication is offered. Such persons may not always be converted; they may resist unto death. It may not be known to others that their minds are exercised at all upon the subject of their sinfulness; they may not know it themselves. Their thought will seem to them natural; and they will attribute it to no unusual cause. The Spirit works in harmony with the laws of mind. Yet all this does not militate against the fact that the prayer of the obedient believer does produce results. When spiritual power is in the soul of the suppliant, and his prayer is perseveringly offered for the glory of God, it is as certainly efficient as any of the forces of nature. Prayer is probably one of the moral forces of the spiritual world.*

The result of prayer may sometimes be judgment mingled with mercies. The spiritual good may begin in some affliction or temporal calamity falling upon a person or a family; some providence needful to produce reflection, or to abate the power of the prince of this world over the soul; but however it begins or advances, where the true Church prays, the Spirit does a work of judgment and mercy, by providence and by truth. The believer will be strengthened, the impenitent awakened, and God will be glorified. If those who are, in such circumstances, enlightened by truth, and "made partakers of the

---

* See Appendix I,— Is Prayer a Moral Force?

heavenly gift," yield their hearts and lives to Christ, they will become sons of God, and will receive the guidance through life of the Pastor and Bishop of the soul. But if, being enlightened, they wickedly resist, occurrences will take place in the seeming natural course of events which will induce scepticism, or in some other way render it more difficult for them ever after to become reconciled to God.*

§ 47.—*Specific work of the Spirit in impenitent minds.*

We come now to notice the work of the Holy Spirit upon the unrenewed mind. The following is the succinct scriptural statement.

John xvi, 8-11, — "When the Comforter is come, he will reprove the world of sin, and of righteousness, and of judgment: Of sin, because they believe not on me; Of righteousness, because I go to the Father and ye see me no more; Of judgment because the prince of this world is judged."

The teaching of this passage, it will be seen, is in precise accordance with what has been

* Heb. vi, 4—.

shown elsewhere to be the *only process* by which man can advance from lower to higher degrees of moral culture and moral character. In order to unity, we will, in this place, recapitulate briefly the statement of those mental necessities* which are met by the Spirit and the truth, as set forth in the above passage.

(1.) "He will convict the world of sin."

It has been shown that there must be a sense of man's guilt and danger existing in the mind before there can be gratitude and love to the being who removes the guilt and rescues from the danger. It has likewise been shown that conviction of sin is a necessary prerequisite to repentance. A man can not conscientiously turn from evil until he sees and feels that it is evil. To suppose that any one will for unselfish reasons turn from a course of life which he does not first feel to be wrong, is to suppose an absurdity. Hence the necessity of the Spirit's

* To the thoughtful there is the highest evidence of the divinity of the New Testament, seen in the harmony of its principles and methods with the laws and necessities of the human mind.

first impression, as stated in the words of Christ, "*He will convict the world of sin.*"

But the same truth would not be adapted to convince all classes of men that they were sinners. Some men are least guilty of sins which are the greatest in the case of others. In order, therefore, to convince any particular class of men of their sinfulness, those facts must be alleged which are adapted to awaken in the soul a sense of personal guilt. In the days of the apostles the Gentiles could not be convicted of sin for rejecting and crucifying Christ; but in the case of the Jews, their views in regard to the Messiah were such, that nothing in the whole catalogue of crime would be adapted to convict them of sin so deeply as the thought that Jesus, whom they had crucified, was the Messiah.

On the contrary, the heathen, upon whom there was no guilt in regard to the rejection of Christ, would be convicted of sin by such revelations of the holiness of God, and the obligation of the moral law, as would condemn their idolatries, impurities and crimes. But in all cases, it was *truth as taught by Christ,* and *judgment as ad-*

ministered by Christ,* which the apostles presented in order to convince the world of sin.

We need not cite instances to show that this was the general order of apostolic proceeding. That quality of truth was used which was adapted to the circumstances and moral attainment of those whom they addressed. The Jews were charged with sin in rejecting Christ. The Gentiles were instructed concerning the true God, the true duty, and the folly and sin of their idolatries; while every where Christ crucified was presented to the penitent sinner as the object of faith, the source of pardon, and the hope of glory.

(2.) "He shall convince the world of righteousness, because I go to the Father, and ye see me no more."

But it requires something more than truth; something more even than acknowledged and adapted truth, to make men feel that they are sinners in *the sight of God*. The Maker, as we have noticed, has so constituted the conscience that it will enforce no truth upon the will unless

* Acts xvii, 31.

there is a sense of God's authority in it. Jesus Himself taught that His truth would not have full spiritual efficacy until after His resurrection. By His resurrection and the advent of the Spirit, as we have shown, the evidence of Divine authority would be given to His teaching. Then it would be empowered to affect the moral nature of man; to become light to the souls of the dark-minded, and life in the souls of those who believe. Hence the second impression of the Spirit by the truth,—" He shall convince the world of righteousness, because I go to the Father, and ye see me no more."

Commentators have blundered even more in regard to the import of this passage than they usually do in regard to the spiritual import of John's gospel. There is no doubt but that it was designed to give the simple *rationale* of the process by which the authority of God was attached to the life and death of Christ. When Christ was raised from the dead and taken to heaven, then the Divine sanction was affixed to His character and instruction, which henceforth became the standard of righteousness. When, under the preaching of the apostles, impressed by the Holy Spirit, men came to believe in the ascension of Christ, as Saviour and Judge of men — then the righteousness of Christ became to them the righteousness that God required, and wanting which they would feel condemned as sinners against God. Hence, men were convinced of righteousness because God established Christ's rule of righteousness by the resurrection from the dead.*

(3.) "He shall convict the world of judgment, because the prince of this world is judged."

Another co-existing conviction promised by the Spirit through the truth was that of judgment or condemnation of the selfish forms and deceptions of a worldly life. Men would see, as soon as they believed that Christ's life was the life that God approved — that the prevailing spirit of the world was condemned by His loving and self-denying example. The selfishness which dictated the factitious manners, and the low and base aims of worldly minds, would be revealed and condemned by the standard of living and the motive of action which Christ had established. This the apostles understood; they taught

---

* See Appendix L, — OLD AND NEW TESTAMENT MORALITY.

that the gospel both revealed sin and condemned it. It led men both to see and to feel the evil of the world. Eph. v, 13,—"*All things that are reproved are made manifest by the light: for whatsoever doth make manifest is light.*"* In the light of the gospel the evil was seen, and by the impression of the Spirit the evil was felt. Thus, in the minds of the sanctified, the ruling spirit of the world was condemned, "the prince of this world was judged."

---

* About the time that Paul wrote the passage from which this quotation is taken, describing the moral corruption which prevailed in the city of Ephesus, Pliny, one of the wisest and most refined men of his age, speaks of the same city as "one of the luminaries of Asia." The one considered her as full of light, the other looked upon her as full of darkness. Both views were true, according to the standard by which the writers formed their judgment. Pliny saw her as the seat of the highest civilization that a people without revelation had attained. But in Paul's mind their impure and immoral deeds were made manifest,—the false external of this world was judged. Underneath the glare of vainglory he saw moral corruption. She was "a whited sepulchre, full of dead men's bones." The description, we fear, is not inapplicable in a moral sense to Paris, New York, New Orleans, Chicago, and some other cities both of the old and the new world. If an angel were to visit the resorts of fashion and wealth, he would frequently see, under the tinsel which opulence furnishes, the corrupt, sensuous, and selfish motives which render the soul a "cage of unclean birds."

§ 48.—*The promised convictions of the Spirit experienced by those who hear the gospel under spiritual impression.*

It has been, in every age since the gospel was first proclaimed, verified in the experience of tens of thousands, that the subjective effects which Christ promised by His Spirit have been produced. Setting aside instances of sympathetic emotion, which do not arise from a sense of heart-guiltiness, and looking charitably upon other movements which may have been produced by sectarian rather than sacred zeal; apart from all such cases, there are multitudes of persons that have felt the convicting power of truth, when that truth has been presented in the presence of Christians whose minds were exercised by faith and prayer. Many have in such circumstances been awakened to see the evil of sin, and to realize the claims of God upon them, with a degree of interest that they never felt before.* The three co-existing impressions—sin,

---

* The writer has seen in two instances respectable business men, from New York city, rise, exercised by a deep sense of sin, to ask the prayers of a congregation in a distant town, after hearing a single sermon, where they knew no one present,

righteousness, and judgment,—promised as the work of the Spirit through the truth, have been produced in their minds. If we converse with friends who are spiritually interested in religious truth, in some respects we may find their exercises different. Some do not feel that in any one particular they have been great transgressors. Many are troubled that they do not *feel* more the guilt of their sins. But notwithstanding diversity of views in regard to their own difficulties and deserts, there is always *the same consciousness of the three-fold impression,*— SIN, RIGHTEOUSNESS, JUDGMENT.

Ask any one of them if they feel that their heart is hard and sinful? Oh yes, they will say, they *see* that, but they do not feel it as they ought. Ask them if they have seen their thoughts to be selfish and evil in the sight of God? Oh yes, they have seen that; and have tried to control their thoughts, and make themselves better, but have failed. They know, they will often tell you, that their heart is in a wrong state, and that they do not feel willing

and no one knew them until subsequent inquiry. No word was said and no prayer uttered except the ordinary service of the Sabbath.

to do the will of Christ. By such statements concerning their exercises it will be apparent to enlightened minds, although it may not be to themselves, that they are convinced of sin; some more deeply than others; but still the consciousness, in kind, is the same. They see the evil of sin, and feel it to some extent. The "I" of the mind, which sees the thought, is convicted, and is opposing selfish exercises and wrong propensities. Like Paul, in the Pharisee state, such persons "consent unto the law that it is good; but when they would do good, evil is present with them."

The second impression also, a sense of righteousness, is found in their mind. It is the perception "that the law is good" that enables them to feel the evil of their heart. They consent to the law, and yet find in themselves a want of conformity to it. They have begun to read the Scriptures and to study righteousness as it is revealed there; and they approve it. They may have had speculative ideas of sin before, and compunction for wrong doing towards others; this, all persons who possess a natural conscience, will sometimes experience. But now they feel—as did David—that they have "*sin-*

ned against God, and done the evil in HIS *sight."* * Their conscience accuses them of ingratitude and disobedience toward their Divine Benefactor. The truth of Scripture has now for them a sense of God in it; and in its light they judge of their past life and their present duty.

And, finally, an awakened mind feels, in a sense difficult to express, that the forms and professions of the world are hollow and selfish. And at this point the issue between Christ and Belial for ascendancy in the soul is usually made. The ties of companionship and the power of worldly habits and associations are strong — so strong, that many who see the danger, and desire a better life, have not sufficient of principle and purpose to emancipate themselves from a service which their awakened conscience condemns. Some look up, and under the impulse of the Spirit, struggle to enter in at the strait gate; while others, of more feeble purpose and less moral principle, "desire — seek to enter in, but are not able."

Thus the three-fold conviction of the Spirit is distinct, notwithstanding the varied exercises

* Ps. li, 4.

caused by different temperaments, histories, degrees of knowledge and degrees of sin. In the case of all adult persons who have lived a selfish life antecedent to conversion, there will be found in their minds the three co-existing impressions — sin, righteousness, judgment — in the sense above described.

§ 49.—*The awakening of the lost sinner, and his return to God, as illustrated by the Lord Jesus.*

The parable of the prodigal son is a beautiful, affectionate, and striking illustration of the convicted consciousness, and the state of mind in which a lost sinner returns to God. That the parallel may be more distinct, we will present the figure and its fact in opposite columns.

The prodigal takes his portion of goods and leaves home to follow his own will and seek his own happiness in a far-off country.	So the son of the Divine Father takes the talents committed to him, and, if not a believer, at the age of responsibility he departs and seeks his own will and his happiness in the world.
The wandering son, having wasted his substance, is sent to feed swine, and is willing to live on swines' food.	The wandering sinner, having wasted his energies in sensual and selfish schemes, seeks to satisfy his soul with earthly and animal good.

No man gave the prodigal, even of the husks he desired. He found no satisfying good in any earthly source ; husks would not satisfy the appetite.

Finally, through the effect of his experience, and by reflection upon his destitute condition, the prodigal " comes to himself," begins to reflect — to realize the danger and want of his present state. He thinks of his father, and of the supplies and peace in his distant home.

The prodigal, after serious thought, says to himself, I will arise — go home, and confess myself a sinner in the sight of God and my father, and say that I am unworthy to be called a son.

The prodigal, in view of his past sin and his unworthiness, is willing to return and labor and be treated *as a hired servant*, feeling that his father will do right if he obeys his

So the sinner tries but fails to make himself happy. He turns from one man to another, and from one thing to another, but nothing temporal will satisfy spiritual wants. It is as husks to the appetite.

So the sinner "comes to himself." He becomes conscious of his present unsatisfied and sinful condition. He thinks of his heavenly Father, and begins seriously to meditate upon his spiritual wants, and the supplies offered in the gospel.

. So the sinner purposes to arise and return to the home of the soul. He feels that he has sinned against heaven and in the sight of God, and that he is unworthy to be called a a son, and often in heart-prayer confesses his sin

So the awakened sinner, after purposing to arise and go to his Father, finally DOES ARISE and goes towards home. He goes feeling he is unworthy, and asking to be made as a will. Thus he returns to obey without making any conditions.

The father sees the prodigal coming at a great distance, and goes out to meet him. The distance is at first great, so that they are some time approaching each other; but they meet, and the father receives the penitent as a son that "was lost but is found."

There was rejoicing in the presence of the father, and among the other servants, when the prodigal returned. His soiled garments were exchanged for clean robes, and a feast of social enjoyment was held to celebrate his arrival at home.

The reason why the father of the prodigal rejoiced was, that his "son who was dead is alive again; he was lost but is found."

hired servant — not demanding the joy and privileges of a son, but willing to obey as a humble penitent, and trust his Father without conditions.

So God sees the sinner at a great distance when he first begins to think of his sin and his duty. He goes out to meet him by His providence and His Spirit. And he who is returning, willing to obey as a servant, is met and received as a son.

So when the penitent sinner returns, "There is joy in the presence of the angels of God." The servants of the Divine Master on earth likewise rejoice. There is social joy in the Church: and the heart of the wanderer is now purified by faith that works by love, and he puts on the garments of righteousness.

So there is joy in heaven — because a soul dead in sin lives now to God; a soul lost to happiness and usefulness, lives to glorify God and benefit men.

Thus has the great promise of the Redeemer been verified — in the history of the Church, in the experience of men, and in harmony with the specific illustrations of the Great Teacher himself. From the day of Pentecost to the present hour, that promise has been fulfilled in the sanctification of saints, and in the conviction and conversion of sinners; and the work will go on increasing in prevalence, purity, and power, until the end of the dispensation. Men may hate the truth and reject the witness, but still "the counsel of God stands sure;" and wherever the truth is preached, men's destiny for mercy or for judgment is connected with the disposition they manifest towards Christ, who comes to them in the influence of the Divine Spirit. 1 John v. 10, — "He that believeth on the Son hath the witness in himself: he that believeth not God, hath made him a liar: because he believeth not the record that God gave of his Son."

§ 50. — *The son's life at home.*

A sense of his lost condition and faith in his father's mercy brought the wanderer home. When he has returned, faith and obedience are the impulse and the law of a happy home life. But some Christians err by supposing that the life of faith is a constant flow of joyful emotion. Sometimes joy is sought with a selfish motive, which opens the mind to deception, or which hinders the peace granted upon unconditional submission to the will of God. Men are so constituted that strong emotion can not be lasting; reaction must follow. "Peace"* is the promise of the Saviour, and to the Christian a permanent peace, hallowed by love, may be enjoyed. This is the believer's privilege in circumstances where there can be no peace to those unreconciled to God. The things of the world with him are subservient to higher interests, and whether circumstances be propitious or adverse, he is still grateful, because he believes that "all things work together for good to those who love God."

The eldest son in the parable had always been at home — had obeyed from his youth; and although it is affirmed that all that the father had was his, yet he could not experience the extreme joy of the returned prodigal, because the sudden change from death to life was no

---

* John xiv, 27 — "Peace I leave with you, my peace I give unto you."

part of his experience. Yet he had the father's favor, and he was the father's heir. So those who from childhood obey God.

But the prodigal son returns to obey the will of his father. The will of God, and not his own will is the law of life with the believer. But while the law is obeyed as a rule of duty, that law is likewise an expression of the will and heart of his Divine Benefactor. Christian life is not therefore, the service of duty under the impulse of conscience alone; the impulse of love is united with the element of conscience. Thus love to men, as the object of effort, and love to Christ, as the author of effort, distinguish the son from the servant in the life of faith.

But still the will of Christ is supreme law with the believer. He passes from the technical righteousness of the formalist, and the imputed righteousness of the dogmatist, to the actual righteousness of the obedient in heart. He can not do any thing deliberately that he knows Christ will disapprove. At home and abroad, in private and in public, a true Christian will do right—right in testimony and right in action. Righteousness is not a technical but a cardinal principle of the gospel. John Huss, John Knox, John Bunyan, Jeremy Taylor, William Penn, the Wesleys, would neither one of them have violated his conscience for the gift of a kingdom. Christ's righteousness made them righteous, not only in name but in fact.

In all things the Christian has faith in God. He believes God hears prayer. He sees the divine hand in all the providences that come to pass, small and great. He knows this is a state of probation, and that in a world of imperfection, where the good and the evil are mingled, the same external providence often befalls both classes. But he is sure nothing will befall *him* without some wise design, either to discipline him for some evil or to remove from him some temptation; and he relies with perfect assurance on the promise that "all things work together for good to those who love God, to those who are the called according to his purpose." The believer's faith transmutes adverse providences into spiritual good. The providence that renders the unreconciled more selfish, sanctifies the believing mind. Thus the truth he believes, the discipline he receives, and the duties he discharges, all combine to fit the Christian for the "inheritance of the saints in light." And when the end comes, *his sense of immortality* is produced by the presence of the Holy Spirit in his soul, and his hope of heaven is not by reason, but by faith in Christ, from whom he consciously draws eternal life, as the branch lives by its union with the vine. Having "fought the good fight and finished his course," he departs to receive the "crown of life, which God, the righteous Judge, will give him at that day, and not to him only, but to all them also that love his appearing."

CHAPTER VIII.

SUPPLEMENTARY.

In the preceding sections on prayer and the Holy Spirit, the exposition does not include all the relations of the subject, and miraculous gifts by the Spirit are not noticed. We here supplement the preceding thoughts by additional sections. The whole, we hope, may form a Scriptural Monograph on the Doctrine of the Holy Spirit—a subject which should be held as of vital religious interest by all believers in the New Dispensation of our Lord and Saviour Jesus Christ.

§ 53.—*The promise of the Holy Spirit in answer to prayer, is in harmony with the method of the gospel, that grace is bestowed upon one in order that benefit may be conferred upon others.*

Jesus prayed frequently, importunately and submissively; and He promised His disciples that, *if they obeyed His commandments*, whatsoever they asked of the Father, regarding Him in the name or character manifested in Christ, would be done for them. They were invited to ask in order that their joy might be full, and in order that they might be qualified to communicate to others the blessing they had received.

The special promise of the New Testament on the subject of prayer is, that prayer for the Holy Spirit will be answered when the believer prays for grace *to enable him to benefit others*, as stated in the passage given in Luke xi. The point and intent of the passage, as stated and illustrated by Jesus,* is not that those who pray for the Holy Spirit shall receive it for their own

---

* "And he said unto them, which of you shall have a friend, and shall go unto him at midnight, and shall say unto him — Friend, lend me three loaves, for a friend of mine, in his journey, has come to me, and I have nothing to set before him. And he from within shall answer and say, — Trouble me not, the door is now shut, and my children are with me in bed; I cannot rise and give thee. I say unto you, though he will not rise and give him because he is his friend, yet because of his importunity he will rise and give him as many as he needeth. And so I say unto you, *Ask, and it shall be given you*" *for your friends.* — Luke xi, 1-14.

spiritual good. This is true in a relative sense. As food taken to give us bodily strength is the order of nature to qualify us for work, so the Spirit gives spiritual strength. But the aim of the benediction is not ultimate with the recipient. The same end for which Christ died is the aim of the endowment—to bless one in answer to prayer, that he may be the instrument of conveying the same blessing to others.

If Christ has a kingdom in this world to be established under God by human agency, then providence and power would be given to accomplish the aim of that kingdom, which is that members of the human brotherhood should be instrumental in saving each other. Thus the analogy of faith sanctions a true exposition.

Now the above construction, which is the scriptural one, brings prayer into accordance with the plan and process of gospel duty, as developed in preceding sections. Christians who desire to follow Christ in labor for human good should understand what expositors have failed to notice — that the unreserved promise of the Holy Spirit in the gospel is predicated upon the fact *that the supplicant seeks grace for himself that he may impart good to others.* The illustration by the

Saviour precedes the promise recorded in the same passage. The promise is the same in Matt. vii, 6–12, where the parable is omitted. The Spiritual import of the passage is plain and impressive. Jesus gives the bread of life, as it is written, "he that eateth of this bread shall never die." The suppliant is deeply interested for his friend, but cannot himself furnish the means of life to the wayfarer on his journey to the judgment. The Saviour is the friend of the suppliant, who goes to Him and seeks importunately for the needed loaves, which he receives in order to convey them to the one for whom he intercedes.

Harmonists generally have supposed that the promise in Matt. vii, and Luke xi, was spoken on different occasions. There is no reason whatever for this division of the text. Besides, if thus divided, the full record elucidates the abbreviated one. If Dr. Robinson had urged one-half the reasons to show that the passages are one that he has to show that the Sermon on the Mount is the same in the two evangelists, the first case would have been more evident than the second. Luke evidently designed to give the whole passage concerning prayer, and to separate it from its contexts in time and place. In the order of the passage likewise the gospel economy requires that the illustration by the parable in Luke should come between the Lord's prayer and the promise of the Holy Spirit. The Lord's prayer is preliminary to duty. It is morning worship and supplication for daily strength, pardon and guidance: (*a*) Let the Divine name — [character — as revealed in Christ] — be hallowed. (*b*) Let the Divine kingdom be established in the earth. (*c*) Give us our daily bread. (*d*) Forgive us our sins, when we forgive others. (*e*) Save us when tempted. (*f*) Deliver from evil influence.— When their devotion had thus risen to the name of God in Christ, when His kingdom had been presented as the first interest, when they had prayed for daily strength and daily mercy, when they had sought the guidance of Providence and succor in temptation — *then*, being thus qualified by personal devotion for personal effort, the illustration in Luke intervenes, and the Holy Spirit is promised to aid the disciple, thus endowed, to communicate spiritual good personally to the friend for whom he prays. Then follows the promise with the connective joining the two passages: "And I say unto you, ask and it shall be given you" —*for the subjects of your prayer.* "Seek"— *with the motive this man had*—"and ye shall find." "Knock"—*for the same purpose*—"and it shall be opened unto you." "For if ye being evil know how to give good gifts to your children, how much more will your Heavenly Father give his Holy Spirit to them that ask him." Give it to bless them first with a satisfying portion, and thus qualify them as mediums to impart the same good to others.

Thus the *unconditional* promise of the Spirit is *conditional* upon the believer asking for the bread of life that he may be the instrument of conveying spiritual good to others.

§ 54.— *The subjects of prayer should be specifically in view of the mind of the suppliant, when he cannot personally communicate with them.*

The New Testament requires us to supply the temporal needs of the children of want as an antecedent to spiritual effort for their good (James ii). The Christian philanthropist is distinguished from others who do good, in that the motive of one ends on the earthly condition of the object, while that of the other makes earthly benefits auxiliary to the spiritual good of the soul. One administers to man as an animal, the other to man as having a higher spiritual nature. But where temporal needs are not in the case, and where absence and other circumstances separate the suppliant from the object of his prayer, then it is an important question whether or not there be a connection in thought between the mind of the suppliant and the subject of his supplication. Intercession for rulers and for the general good of the State and society is, no doubt, a duty; but even in such cases it may be supposed that the persons and the ends desired are in the mind of the suppliant. But it is very questionable, from Bible premises, and from many marked cases of answer to prayer,* whether the law of impression upon one mind in accordance with the prayer of another which is energized by the Holy Spirit, does not require the special personal interest of the suppliant for the object of his intercession. The case of the text for the wayfarer in life's journey — the prayers for Peter

* See notes at the end of the chapter.

in prison, indeed all the Scripture cases, directly or indirectly, imply that the objects of prayer were pressing upon the minds of the suppliants.

If there be truth in this exposition two things are required — first, that the suppliant has himself spiritual endowment from the Lord; and, second, that the object of his intercession should be a special interest upon his mind when he prays.

If these views are warranted, then those requests presented at the Fulton street prayer meeting, and other christian assemblages, which speak in such general language as this: *Prayer is requested for a certain man in Rochester, or at Natchez, or at the West, who is becoming intemperate,*—such requests give no direction to the minds of those who pray; and the supplication offered cannot be under the guidance of the Holy Spirit, who indicates subjects of prayer and gives impression in regard to those subjects. The fact that such a request is presented shows that some Christian mind has a spirit of prayer for the subject referred to, and good may reach him, although not through the indefinite supplication requested.

§ 53.— *The miraculous gifts of the Holy Spirit were not the product of the Indwelling Spirit, in the ordinary sense.*

There were occasions when the life and labors of the apostles were guarded by a special Providence, and when miraculous powers were exerted as testimony to others, that God approved their ministry. Gifts of healing, knowledge of future events, and the abused gift of tongues, were among these. Such manifestations were Divine interpositions, on special occasions, through the apostles, rather than the normal manifestations of their internal spiritual life. These miraculous interventions, granted only in certain exigencies, were to cease, while the indwelling Spirit was to remain with believers until the end of the dispensation.

The gift of tongues is one of the most difficult subjects which an interpreter finds in the New Testament. Whether the annunciation of the foreign language at Pentecost was by the magnetic current from the brain of the apostles, which appeared as tongues, separated into two points, like flame, upon their heads; or whether it was through their proper organs of speech, or both, we have now no way of determining. Subsequently, it is evident, no such tongues of flame appeared, and the exercise of this gift was discouraged. So much so was this the case, that Paul had to admonish the churches not to forbid it altogether. With the limited permission granted by the apostle these were conditions which excluded all fanatical utterances: — such utterances, perhaps, of sincere enthusiasts as those who, in the days of Edward Irving, spoke in unintelligible voices which they believed were given by the Holy Ghost. The apostle limited the utterance to words which would edify the church, and urged his own reticence as an example to restrain the practice in others. The gift of tongues was not one of the promised gifts of the Spirit, hence its manifestation and history differ from other supernatural endowments promised by the Lord. Tongues were for a sign, and on the day of Pentecost they were a special aid in introducing the gospel.

But there were specific promises in regard to the miraculous manifestations of the Holy Spirit, as there were in regard to its fruits in the souls of believers. One of the transcendent gifts promised, was that, to some of the disciples, in certain cases, the events of the future would be made known. "He will show you things to come." Hence, Stephen was put to death for affirming that God would destroy the city of Jerusalem, and change the institutions established by Moses. Paul informed the captain of the vessel endangered by the storm that the crew would be saved. Agabus informed Paul of the bonds and imprisonment that awaited him at Jerusalem. And both Paul and Peter distinctly delineated the features of the incoming Papal apostasy, that ruled the darkness during the eclipse of the written Word in the dark ages.

The gift of healing was likewise promised in connection with the commission to preach the gospel. It was not accomplished at will by the grace of the indwelling Spirit, but was exercised through the disciples, in answer to their supplication, and as exigences might require. Hence the disciples pray (Acts iv, 30), "Grant unto thy servants boldness to speak the word, by stretching forth thy hand to heal, and that signs and wonders may be done in the name of thy holy child Jesus." While the apostles, therefore, realized their dependence upon miraculous interposition for prestige and acceptance in cases of exigency, they recognized the fact that the power, as to time and place, was in the hands of God.

There was an intelligent discrimination made, by the first disciples, between the life of the indwelling Spirit and those acts of power which God accomplished through their agency. For the agency which they exerted in connection with the promptings of the Spirit they felt themselves responsible. Hence the precepts, "walk in the Spirit,"—"be filled with the Spirit,"—"praying in the Spirit,"—"grieve not the Holy Spirit of God." But miraculous agency was subject to the Divine will, and although exerted for them and through them, the power, as to time and place, was above their control,—was exercised only on special occasions, and might be exercised through any agent, or upon any subject, according to need and use.

The light of human experience in all ages, more especially in less enlightened ages and places, will enable us to appreciate some peculiar statements in apostolic history on this subject. It is stated that when these miracles of healing had excited the minds of the people, the enthusiasm awakened, together with the hope of healing for themselves or their friends, led many into superstitious practices, such as often occur in similar cases. The persons of the apostles were looked upon as the sources of healing. Some brought the sick and laid them where the shadow of Peter in passing might fall upon them. Others brought scarfs and handkerchiefs to the diseased that had touched the person of Paul. And at Lystra, the priests of Jupiter could scarcely be restrained from offering sacrifices to Paul and Barnabas, in consequence of the miracle of healing performed in their city.

That many cases of healing occurred in such connection, by the influence which it is known an excited mind exerts upon the body, was doubtless true; and it may have been, as in like cases, that the apostles had no conscious influence in the matter. The influence of the imagination to affect the body physically has not yet ceased in the world; and in darker ages the effect was in proportion to the strength of superstition among the people. Hence the scripture narrative not only accords with the supernatural, but with natural relations in that age.

§ 54.—"*The prayer of faith shall save the sick, * * * and if he have committed sins they shall be forgiven.*"

It is asked why the efficacy of prayer has ceased, or why Paul left a companion at Miletus sick, if there were gifts of healing that could be exercised at pleasure? There is no satisfactory answer to such questions unless we find the moral principle which governed in such cases. All sicknesses originate in natural causes; but in some cases they likewise have a moral connection, coming as a penalty for sin. It is a Bible principle, that those who have faith in God suffer in this life if they sin, whilst the disobedient are reserved for judgment until the future life. Hence sickness and other adverse providences often come as discipline in the case of believers who have committed offences against God of which they have not repented. The sicknesses removed by the prayer of faith belonged to this category.

The suffering of believers is made available to their moral good. Both their own personal affliction and the suffering of Christ are means of sanctification to those who have faith. Faith sees the hand of God in the affliction, and connects it with themselves in a moral sense; hence the dispensation makes them more humble — more obedient — more holy. A true faith always transmutes physical evil to moral good. Thus the Christian is sanctified by affliction, and freed from the love and practice of sin, which would alienate the mind from God and produce future evil. As it is said in Scripture, 1 Cor. xi, 32, — " When we are judged, we are chastened of the Lord, that we should not be condemned with the world." But the unregenerated are " reserved until the day of judgment to be punished." It would not be a benefit to the earthly-minded to punish them here. It would be adding providential evil to natural evil without benefit to the sufferer. It could do them no spiritual good, *because it is faith alone that transmutes present evil to an everlasting benefit.*

The application of the principle is distinctly revealed in connection with the church of Corinth. The converts there, recently redeemed from heathenism, had fallen into abuses of the Lord's Supper. They had turned a sacred memorial into a bacchanal feast. Hence many were under discipline, by debility and disease, and some had died. 1 Cor. xi, 30,—" For this cause many are weak and sickly among you, and many sleep." They were under the discipline of affliction because of their sin, and some were dead, because, perhaps, if they had lived they would have grown worse; and hence it was benevolence that called them from a life which they were likely to abuse. Just as some churches are benefited when God takes their ministers to heaven (if indeed they go there), because they get a better man.

Now those afflicted persons who were benefited by prayer and medical appliances administered in faith, were believers—Christians who were suffering discipline for the indulgence of some sin, an affliction of which perhaps these sinful indulgences were the natural cause; as in the case of the Corinthians, whose debility and suffering had no doubt its origin in their bibulous excesses. Hence, when the sin was repented of—as the suffering came as a consequence, both naturally and morally—the cause and its consequences would be removed together.

So in other like cases. It is stated in the context that the repentance of the sufferer was a concomitant in the removal of the affliction.

Then the prayer of faith would save the sick, and all would glorify God for His goodness. By the repentance of the subject, the aim of the discipline would be gained; and by departing from his sin the natural cause of the disease would be removed; and by faith the Church would see the goodness of God in the recovery of the sick. Hence it is added in the passage, "If he has committed sin it shall be forgiven him." The end of the discipline is attained, the moral effect aimed at is accomplished, and the sick man recovers according to both the natural and moral economy of the Divine government.

Whether such interposition by providential agency be necessary in the present state of the Church, others may judge. It would at least be well if intelligent physicians, who have learned enough to know that medical appliances are seldom of much value, had more faith in the power of the Great Physician, who, in accordance with preceding views, removed bodily maladies in order that men might believe that He had power to remove the malady of the soul. (See Matt. ix, 6.)

§ 55.—*Was the Spiritual endowment imparted by laying on of hands to be transient or permanent in the churches?*

Laying on of hands seems to have been understood in the primitive churches as an impartation of spiritual influence from the minds of those in sympathy with Christ, to those who received the benediction. In the sixth chapter of the Epistle to the Hebrews it is given as one of the circle of foundation doctrines in the Christian system. The translators, by imperfect punctuation, have somewhat blinded its import. The passage, expounded according to the analogy of faith, is as follows: "Advancing from the first principles of the gospel of Christ, which we accepted at our initiation, let us go onward to perfection, not laying over again the foundation principles, which are: (1) *Repentance*, or turning from *dead* works—*i. e.*, works without love—to works produced by faith in Christ. (2) *Faith* towards God as manifest in the flesh. (3) *Baptisms*, or purification by the Holy Ghost, and its symbol water baptism. (4) The *laying on of hands;* to communicate spiritual influence to qualify for official labor in the Church of

God. (5) *The resurrection of the dead.* (6) *Eternal judgment.*

Of these six foundation tenets the laying on of hands is the fourth. It was certainly one of the recognized ordinances of the Gospel according to the conception of those who founded the christian institutions. *That with them it implied the communication of the Holy Spirit as that Spirit energized in the souls of the administrators, there is no room for doubt.* It becomes, therefore, an inquiry of deep importance whether the accompanying grace of the Holy Spirit, imparted by the laying on of hands, was one of those gifts which was to cease with the founders of the New Testament Dispensation, or whether it was to continue as an efflux of Spiritual influence, imparted from gracious minds to others approved of God as gospel ministers?

There are well informed observers who think that after all the apocryphal or doubtful views of mesmerism are rejected, there is still sufficient evidence to believe that at the present time, as in all past times, the logos of one mind may, in certain pathological conditions, be transferred to another. Dr. Carpenter, the best living physiologist, assents to this view. To such as suppose miracles are not in contravention of natural law, such testimony may aid conviction. But apart from the deductions of physiology and psychology, there are scriptural and rational considerations in regard to this subject to which prayerful christians ought to take heed. These we think favor the conclusion that the benediction imparted by the laying on of hands, was an efflux of the indwelling Spirit, rather than an exercise of miraculous power.

(*a*) It is spoken of as one of the fundamental principles of Christianity. It is agreed that the other five were to continue in the church to the end of time — the same in import and efficacy as at the beginning. Can any good reason be adduced for making the laying on of hands an exception?

(*b*) The same hortatory instructions are applicable in this case as in other cases of the indwelling Spirit — the difference being only in the degree and the characteristics of the power imparted. Hence the exhortation of Paul to Timothy: "Neglect not the gift that is in thee, which was given thee by prophecy and by the laying on of 'hands' of the Presbytery." In this case the apostle affirms that the elders of the church imparted the gift, and the young preacher is called upon to exercise his agency in coöperation with the inward grace.

(c) The Spirit was conferred in connection with belief of the truth. Truth is the instrumentality by which the indwelling Spirit operates to glorify God and produce spiritual good in men. Christ is the Truth, and His Spirit is the "Spirit of Truth." Men are born of the Truth, and sanctified by the Truth; hence when the disciples of John were instructed in the fundamental elements of Christian truth — and not till then — they received the Spirit by the laying on of the apostle's hands.

There are certainly reasons for the inquiry whether the churches of our day, conceive of the indwelling Spirit, in believers, and its communications to fit men for particular labors, as did the early disciples. Everything of Divine excellence can be misdirected or perverted, hence there may be danger of a certain kind in urging the evidence on this subject. Formalists and Simonists, and enthusiasts, may profess to communicate Spiritual grace, while the only spirit that is in them is earthly and selfish. But ought not men of prayer and inward grace to hope that the administration of this ordinance to persons who seek to glorify Christ in their life and ministry, will not be an empty form. but will be accompanied by an "unction from the Holy One"—a spiritual energy indwelling and yet diffusive that will be in some wise subject to the agency of the recipient—and will enable him to "preach the gospel with the Holy Ghost sent down from heaven?"

§ 56.—*Recondite laws of human nature connect themselves with this subject.*

Before our closing illustrations, a thought or two in regard to some profound natural relations of the body and spirit may give completeness to this monograph of the operation of the Spirit of God.

There is in nature what may be called, for want of a better definition—*a sympathetic virtus*—meaning thereby a quality of human nature which, when the soul is excited, causes it to impart of the spirit of its exercises to other minds. It may arise from, and be a proof of the solidarity of the human family, that an excited cord in the mind of one vibrates in others. If this is a characteristic of the nature of mankind, it is open to both evil and good influences, and as God imparts good according to the laws of the nature He has given to man, He would work through these laws in communicating His grace from those nearest Christ to the more remote. We say through those nearest Christ, because the dispensations of the Holy Spirit come to us, as before stated, through the humanity of Jesus. If therefore this *sympathetic virtus* exists in human nature it existed in Christ, and hence the operations of His spirit would partake of its qualities.*

This characteristic of our nature will, of course, manifest itself in an awakened state of the religious sensibility — whether the revival of interest partake mostly of human or of Divine impulse. A pure revival of religion, which always produces "repentance" and restores "first love," will *necessarily* partake of the marks of the Divine indwelling Spirit, as deduced in preceding sections: Not undue excitement, but peace; Duty, which is not labor, but rest; Righteous-

---

* Some man in the future, when this subject is better understood, will show that this quality of human nature is a reason why the Divine mercy should be manifested through the flesh.

ness, which redresses wrong and produces Christian integrity; Faith, which works by love and casts out of the mind personal enmities and alienations.

Men who have spiritual life impart of their human characteristics with the impartations of the Spirit diffused by them. We knew a church once that made decided progress in righteousness and love during a revival of religion. There was one man among the people who possessed the presence of Christ in his heart, and who loved and obeyed as the rule of his life. At home and abroad, in labor or in social life, he did always what he thought would please the Redeemer. During the progress of the interest in the church he was earnest but peaceful. He had unction and humility. As the interest advanced it took on something of the aspect of this faithful man's exercises. It was peaceful, purifying, quickening. It was his custom to give all his means, except a comfortable support for his family, to the cause of Christ.

This religious interest tended strongly in this direction. It produced a conviction of duty that doubled the benevolent offerings of the members of that church from that day forward, and gave a spirit of honesty and charity to professing Christians where before these qualities were deficient. He was an intelligent man; he seemed naturally to oppose whatever injured others. He was intimate with pious people and with all who labored to do good; but rather recluse, although not separate from the more worldly social class. The pastor of the church had evidence to believe that the spiritual graces of this disciple of the Lord was a source of power that reached his own mind and that of others; and the influence of which will never cease.

NOTES

ILLUSTRATING SOME PHASES OF SPIRITUAL COMMUNICATION.

I.

The following statement is made by Rev. R. H. Will, of Illinois, a Methodist minister, in whose integrity all may confide. If such cases were collected by those who have personal knowledge of their occurrence, it would be difficult to assign them to the category of "extraordinary coincidences."

"In a family whose name was Taylor, residing in England, the mother was known as a woman of unusual piety. She had a large family of children. It was her daily habit to take these children into her room and read a portion of Scripture and pray for each of them severally. They were all, as she hoped, converted at an early age, except the youngest one, whose name is George. This one resisted her entreaties, and seemed to pay no heed to her supplication. From youth to manhood he grew more obstinate and reckless, and terminated his connection with his home by enlisting, as a common soldier, in the English army. The mother was grieved, but did not despair. The company into which her son had enlisted was ordered to Quebec, in Canada; but she continued, at the same hour each day, to pray specially for him, as she had for her other children. His course, however, in Canada, where I then resided, as far as the restraints of a soldier's life would permit, was unsteady, and disorderly, and profane.

"On a certain Sabbath day, the mother knew not why, she was strongly impressed to pray for her absent son, and asked her friends in the church to unite with her in special prayer for the salvation of her youngest son, George, then a common soldier in Quebec, of whose case her friends were acquainted. They met and prayed unitedly, and specially that the young man might be 'snatched as a brand from the burning.'

"*At the same hour*, as nearly as could be ascertained, the young man was in a drinking saloon, with companions as violent and wicked as himself. His statement is, that an undefined sense of fear and sin came to him, so that he felt he must leave the place, which he did, intending to go to his barracks. On his way home, seeing a church door open and hearing singing, he entered the place, and in the agony of his mind cried for mercy to God. That night he became a new man. His companions ridiculed and persecuted him for weeks. He labored for their salvation individually, and when I last knew the company all but about twenty professed discipleship to Christ. R. H. WILL."

II.

We know a man who has passed through the common experiences of a busy and successful life, whose spiritual experiences have been, to his own mind, an illustration and confirmation of some of the modes of Divine communication spoken of in the preceding pages. He was reared in a family who were reverent towards God, and strict in the observance of the Sabbath, and in conscientious regard of the duties due to their fellow-men, albeit, like others in the old Scotch churches, they made no opposition to innocent social recreations. At an early age, this man had ideas of God and religion; although when a young man he was sceptical—not concerning God, but concerning revelation—for a number of years. Yet during this period, although the social gayeties of the world were freely accepted, there was an intuitive regard for the Sabbath, and an indisposition to a profane or vicious course of life.

Among the recollections of this man, there is a distinct remembrance of two unusual spiritual experiences before the age of manhood—the first when almost a child, the second after doubt had unwillingly come to his mind. Both these experiences began on the Sabbath. The first, when about thirteen years of age, was an experience of delightful peace of mind. There was a sense of God and duty in it, although this was not measured by any form of faith. The lad recognized it as "religion," and spoke of it as such to his child companions; and they spoke to each other of him as having "become religious." How long this complacency in God lasted is not remembered; but it was a period of days, if not weeks.

The second experience was of a different character. He was conscious of God but not of peace. He was sceptical in regard to the Scriptures, but he rose from his bed in the night and prayed earnestly that, if his doubts were wrong, he might be led to the truth. He felt sinful and unrestful, not in view of the future, but from a sense of God's presence. After a season this unusual consciousness likewise passed away, and no renewal of either state occurred again until the time when he was, as he hoped, "renewed in the spirit of his mind." From the time of the second experience to the income of the new life there were years of study and work, with no conscious change of conviction or character at the time; but afterwards he saw plainly that the sense of God and duty became less influential as years had passed by.

After some years of business life he was providentially thrown into associations where the influences of prayer and piety were prevalent. This was, for him, a new phase of society. For a season he gave no heed, and felt no impression; but there came to him afterwards a deep consciousness of sin — not sin in connection with past life so much as sin in the character of his own spontaneous exercises; and because he felt unwilling to be what he knew he should be. He saw in his heart ingratitude to God in regard to past events, which he had not so considered before. He saw selfishness and evil imaginations as he had not seen them before. After months of unrest — not in view of future punishment, of which he never had a fearful apprehension, but in view of the evil of his own selfish exercises, he passed into a state of conscious peace. Immediately connected with this transition was a sense of the presence of God in nature and in providence. This sense of the Divine produced an elevated and delightsome state of mind. Something in the soul reluctated against any unrighteous or selfish or lustful thought. Theological doctrines were not important — even the doctrine of God in Christ was not so distinct as it afterwards became. The New Testament had a new meaning, and the preacher a new life. Although he loved to live, at this time he was consciously not afraid to die; and he still remembers expressions of surprise from friends when he stated that he did not fear death. And yet he had no distinct apprehension of what the future life is, except that those who die in the Lord have His presence and favor. Thus for many months there was pleasing peace—less in the morning than as the day advanced. He remembers once feeling, like Paul, that he could suffer privation, if thereby others might be brought truly to love and obey the Lord Jesus Christ; and although he had at the time in his mind no analytical view of God manifest in the flesh, yet, when he first heard Christ preached in this hallowed state of mind, he leaned his head forward on the pew, and tears flowed freely, no one knowing of his emotion but himself. The state of mind was the same delightsome consciousness as that of his early boyhood.

After many months of this pleasant inward life, the cares of this world gradually intervened, and the common christian experience superseded the life on the mount. There was still a sense of God in Providence and in Christ; but sins of omission and selfish motive were not so carefully avoided as before. He still lived, in a general sense, to please Christ, but conscience was not so complacent as formerly, and peace and love were not so prevalent as in past days.

At times, during this man's later years, a recurrence for limited seasons of the first peaceful trust was experienced. But it was not the habitual state of mind. Perhaps something in nature or providence prevents this in some cases. But what might have been, if the doctrine of the indwelling Spirit had been taught as the apostles taught it, can not now be known.

Suffice it to say, that the Scripture doctrine,—"Know ye not that the Holy Ghost dwells in you, except ye be reprobates," was not expounded, nor apparently experienced, as it was in the earliest periods of the Christian Church; nor as William Penn, Jeremy Taylor, John Wesley, Jonathan Edwards, and other worthies expounded and experienced it.

Subsequent passages in this gentleman's spiritual history will perhaps throw light upon another phase of the subject. Traveling once with a friend who constantly possessed the presence of the Spirit in his soul, they tarried midway in their journey at a farm house, and occupied the same bed during the night. When he arose the next morning, his soul was possessed of the same delightful peace which had been experienced in former years. He rose before his companion, and went out into the orchard, when nature again seemed to speak of God, and his mind was peaceful and praiseful, as in other days.

On a subsequent occasion, during a special meeting of Christians in a western city, he retired to rest with a graduate from Oberlin, where the presence of the Holy Spirit has been experienced as no where else in the nation. This man's heart was full of zeal for the Lord. The next morning, after a sound sleep, the same spiritual consciousness manifest in the Oberlin student inspired in a measure, the mind of the gentleman who shared his bed; and both spoke with earnestness and devotion in the assemblage they had convened to attend.

Now, we shall make no effort to explain or apply these facts. The person spoken of had, so far as he was conscious, no agency in producing the states of mind described. Hence the influence of the imagination was not a factor in the case. His companions may have prayed for him on those nights. This may be, in part, or wholly, the exposition of the case ; but he had no anticipation of these experiences *when* they came, nor *as* they came. They were generally alike, and like former spiritual experiences, varied only by prevailing interest in some subjects of religious import rather than others.

It is not to be inferred from the foregoing that when persons in common cases are brought into contact with the spiritually minded, that thereby spiritual efficacy is always imparted. Experience teaches otherwise. Some natures are more impressible than others ; and the spiritual and the natural coöperate in the economy of the gospel. But if one who had knowledge of the truth, and desired to obey Christ, lacked spiritual impulse and unction, and if it be the Divine method that the influence of the Holy Spirit is radiated from those who pray to those who need, and in specific cases to qualify them for specific labor, then the bearing of such experiences as the foregoing, in connection with prayer, should be studied and understood.

APPENDIX.

A.

HARMONY BETWEEN GENESIS AND GEOLOGY.

If the visional theory of reconciling the Mosaic and Geological Cosmogonies is to be accepted, some modifications in the views of harmonists, as usually propounded, ought to be admitted. We will propose a modification which we think is more in accordance with the text, and with the requirements of geological facts, than the usual exposition.

The elements of a vision must be composed of the material of preceding thought — of ideas previously in the mind. Hence no idea that had not been conceived of in a waking state by the seer, could enter into the composition of his vision.

Now, the multitudinous life in the primeval sea is implied in the statement that the life-giving Spirit "brooded over the waters." It is likewise implied in the statement that "there was light" before the first day. This life in the waters, however — in twilight, or mingled light and dark — had no connection with the future man. And as it was not an object of vision, no idea of it could exist in a human mind, and hence it would form no part of the panorama which passed before the mind of the seer. The whole paleozoic life-period, therefore, ought to be excluded from the vision, and from the first day-period of the Creation.

Then, in the first chapter of Genesis, the first day begins, not at the beginning of the second verse, *but in the middle of the fourth.* This division, as we shall see, both the phraseology and the sense of the text require. Then the brooding of the life-begetting Spirit and the creation of light, in the paleozoic age, will be excluded from the day-periods, and thrown back to a point indefinitely anterior to the first day. Life in the vision will then properly begin with *the first visible life*, that is, with the vegetation which formed the prominent aspect of the carboniferous series, the first product of creation that is economically connected with man.

Upon a reconsideration of the subject, I think the learned will accept this construction. There are plain reasons for beginning the first day-period at the middle of the fourth verse: among others the following:

1. The preceding words, "God saw the light that it was good," indicate in the usual way the end of a period; a period signalized by the creation of light, *before the division of light and darkness* — a division *by which the first day was produced*, and before which day did not exist.

2. The day-periods are composed of evening and morning, or a division of light and darkness, which, however, did not exist until after the process which begins at the middle of the fourth verse. And when the division had been made — *not before* — the light is called "day." To extend the first day-period, therefore, further back than the middle of the fourth verse, would be to give it a place before the act of God, which constituted it, had been put forth.

3. By this arrangement, which a correct apprehension of the visional theory and of the text both require, a better harmony is produced than a reasoning Christian or an unreasonable skeptic would expect. All life, animal and vegetable, indicated by the brooding of the Spirit, and the existence of light in the paleozoic age, is placed anterior to the first day — where the date of

Moses begins. This dim past furnishes a field without well defined limits, where the transcendental reason may revel amid the first obscure indication that there is a God. And the development of creative energy through the subsequent revealed periods of the earth's progress comes into such harmony with the deductions of science as will be more satisfactory — perhaps a little surprising — to the merely scientific enquirer. A harmony which can be accounted for in no way if the divine guidance in the vision of Moses is rejected, except by supposing that accurate geological knowledge not only existed in Egypt, but that it was developed by the same induction of facts which forms the basis of the science in our own time

B.

(Chap. II, p. 26.)

ANTHROPOPATISM.

NEANDER (Dr. Aug.) assumes this conclusion, although the process by which he reaches it is not given. He says (Church Hist. chap. i.),— " Philo was perfectly right in combating the sensuous anthropopathism of certain Jewish Rabbis. But here, as it often happens, in avoiding one error he fell into another of an opposite character, by mistaking and overlooking the objective and *real truths* which were at the *groundwork* of that anthropopathical form in which they were delivered — a form necessary not only to the multitude in early ages, but *to man, as man*, WHO CAN ONLY CONTEMPLATE THE DIVINE, UNDER THE ANALOGY, DEFINED INDEED AND ENNOBLED, BUT STILL THE ANALOGY OF THE HUMAN."

In accordance with the necessities of our limited human mind was the manifestation of God in the flesh. In the future, when philosophy shall have escaped from the shadows in which she has been enveloped by the transcendentalists, or dogmatic intuitionists (we do not speak invidiously) there will come a man who will demonstrate better than we have done, that by a manifestation in humanity alone can the divine be revealed to the human. Anthropology, as the only method of divine manifestation, has its laws, which are all fulfilled by the incarnation of the Logos.

So Cousin, in Lecture Sixteen, on the True, Beautiful, and Good, says, " God is the type of the moral personality that we carry in us. Man is a moral personality; that is to say, he is endowed with reason and liberty. He is capable of virtue, and virtue has, in him, two principal forms, regard for others and love for others — justice and charity.

" Can there be among the attributes possessed by the creature something essential not possessed by the Creator? Whence does the effect draw its reality and its being, except from its cause? What it possesses it borrows and receives. The cause, at least, contains all that is essential in the effect. What particularly belongs to the effect is inferiority — a lack — an imperfection. From the fact alone that it is dependent and derived, it bears in itself the signs and conditions of dependence. If, then, we can not legitimately conclude from the imperfection of the effect, that of the cause, we can and must conclude from the excellence of the effect in the perfection of the cause, otherwise there would be something prominent in the effect, which would be without cause.

"Such is the principle of our theodicea. It is neither new nor subtle; but it has not yet been thoroughly disengaged and elucidated, and it is, to our eyes, firm against every test. *It is by the aid of this principle that we can, up to a certain point, penetrate into the true nature of God.*"

C.

(Chap. III., p. 42.)

THE SCIENTIFIC FORMULÆ OF THE BIRTH OF CHRIST.

SKEPTICAL minds have imagined more difficulties than really exist in connection with the manner of Christ's birth. Difficulties may easily be alleged, and yet if a Christ were born at all, whose nature was in advance of the present human species (as that of a Christ must necessarily be), the analogies of science would determine that his conception and birth would be in accordance with the statement of the Scriptures.

Almost all naturalists who have studied the fossil species as they succeed each other in the geological history of our globe, have supposed that the introduction of each new species was an immediate act of creation. Whether the new form with its faculties were produced by gestation in a lower species, or in some other way, it is generally agreed that the life-power of the new form was introduced by the immediate agency of the Creator. So it is in regard to the two moral species, the Adamic and the Christian, (1 Cor. xv, 45-48), The first man Adam was made a living soul; the last Adam a life-giving Spirit. Howbeit [in the process of development] "that was not first which is spiritual, but that which is natural; and afterwards that which is spiritual. The first man is of the earth, earthy: the second man is the Lord from heaven. As is the earthy, such are they also that are earthy: and as is the heavenly, such are they also that are heavenly." That is, Adam is the head of an inferior species, whose supreme motive and supreme end lie in the earth. Christ, the second Adam, is the head of a superior species, whose motives and end are spiritual, above the earth. Hence " that which is born of the flesh is flesh, that which is born of the Spirit is spirit." Christ, as the Son of Man, was a new species of the human genus, and the type and head of His species. The germ of the new creature is imparted by regeneration, and developed out of the old Adamic nature; and in the resurrection, the corporeity of those in whom is the image of Christ will be developed into "the likeness of Christ's glorified body." "We shall awake in his likeness." Hence the birth of Christ, as the first of a superior species of the *genus homo;* and the promises, to those who have spiritually "put on the new man in Christ Jesus," are in accordance with the order of the Divine working in nature, and with the law of progress which has ruled in the processes of creative energy from the beginning.

D.

(Chap. IV., p. 54.)

PAUL, NOT MATTHIAS, THE TWELFTH APOSTLE.

The Apostle Paul was by education and natural endowment especially qualified for the work of teaching the gospel to the powerful and the learned. The other eleven were men from the masses, and fitted to gain sympathy and feel sympathy with them. Paul (one in twelve) was learned in Jewish and Grecian literature; and he was called to his work after the foundations had been laid at the bottom of society by the other apostles. Reformations always begin near the bottom of society and work upwards. The highest and the lowest are the most depraved circles, excepting always the criminals, who are enemies of all society. Hence it follows that spiritual religion generally reaches the upper circles in Church and State last of all. But still some rich and noble are called up to the meekness of the gospel, and Paul was the man to call such to repentance. He was a man of means, of character, and of culture; and hence his agency was needed to bring the truth before the educated classes of his time. He was a sincere Jew, according to Moses, having passed in his experience from a state of natural religion, or the patriarchal, to a state of conviction by the law — to the Pharisee state, in which he sought for salvation, as many do now, by ritual observances — the state which Luther had reached when he found the Bible at Erfurth. Paul's religious propensions, his sincerity, his culture, fitted him, when endued with the Spirit, for an extraordinary place in the company of the apostles. To fill this place, Jesus personally chose him to the apostleship. Forgiven, because he had ignorantly persecuted believers, supposing that he was doing God service — called from the midst of the shekinah by the voice of Christ; when a suitable time had passed for the tumult of thought to subside, and prayer and reflection to supervene, he was instructed and converted, and then, without "consulting flesh and blood," he began the great labor of his life, — a labor by which, "being dead, he yet speaketh."

As before stated, his special commission is declared, and his commission given; Acts ix, 15, 16,—"He is a chosen vessel unto me, to bear my name before Gentiles, and kings, and the children of Israel; and I will show him how great things he shall suffer for my sake." He, too, "had seen Christ, as one born out of due time," and was chosen, Acts xxii, 15, "to be a witness to all men of what he had seen and heard."

Paul claimed to be an apostle in the same sense in which the other eleven were apostles. Some, it seems, had doubted his apostolic authority; hence to the Corinthians he says (1 Cor. ix, 2), "If I be not an apostle to others, yet doubtless I am to you: for the seal of mine apostleship are ye in the Lord." And again, (2 Cor. xi, 5), "For I suppose that I am nothing behind the very chiefest of the apostles."

He administered discipline in the name, and by the authority, of an apostle. 1 Cor. v, 3–5, —"For I verily, as absent in body, but present in spirit, have determined already, as though I were present, concerning him that hath done this deed, In the name of our Lord Jesus Christ, to deliver such an one unto Satan for the destruction of the flesh, that the spirit may be saved in the day of the Lord Jesus."

He likewise ordained pastors or bishops in the churches, and imparted the Holy Spirit by the laying on of his hands.

Another special mark of apostleship, promised by the Saviour, was, that they should "go forth, and bear fruit, and that their fruit should remain." Paul's epistles are numerous and spiritual. They "remain," a permanent fruit of his life, in the churches. They were recognized as Scripture by the apostles themselves (2 Pet. iii, 15, 16), and they will be received as Holy Scripture till the end of the world.

Finally, God, by His Spirit and His providence, recognized Paul as an apostle, enduing him with apostolic gifts and graces, delivering him from enemies, and working in him and through him for the detachment of the new dispensation from the old, to which believing Jews then adhered, as many modern Christians still do, with the utmost tenacity.

Several things may be learned from the haste of Peter in acting without the promised Spirit, and the subsequent call of Paul by the Lord Jesus Christ himself.

Ordination, where there is no Holy Spirit, is not scriptural ordination. The laying on of hands by men who do not possess the spirit of Christ themselves, is not consecration. Hence, offices and interests imparted by men or churches whose spirit is merely formal and secular, have no Divine validity. The men appointed under such circumstances may be good and useful, as many of them are. Communications of grace from above may be granted them. But the seal of God is not in the act of ordination. And Paul, called of God, with only the right hand of fellowship given him by the apostles, does the work of God better than Matthias, ordained by non-spiritual administrators.

E.

(Chap. V., p. 102.)

THE SOURCE OF FANATICISM.

THE want of a clear perception of the doctrine that the Holy Spirit does not speak of Himself—does not teach any new thing—has been a fruitful source of disorder and fanaticism in all ages. Some who have claimed to be led by the Spirit have forgotten that the Spirit leads only by the truth which Christ revealed in the New Testament. The Spirit brings truth to remembrance, but it is by the law of suggestion—and it is " all things whatsoever Christ said "—not new truth or revelation to individuals. The Spirit can not bring to remembrance truth that was never in the mind, *hence instruction in truth is in order to the work of the Spirit*. Moreover, persons who claim to be moved by the Holy Spirit ought not to forget that " the spirit of the prophets is subject unto the prophets." Paul could speak with tongues more than all others, yet he would not do it, and seems to censure those who did.

The sure point of fanaticism is when an individual claims that his mind is passively controlled by Divine influence. If the Spirit controls the will of the subject in worship or duty, it is not the free responsible subject worshiping God, but God worshiping and obeying Himself. The precepts of the New Testament in regard to the Spirit are all addressed to the human agent. "Walk in the Spirit." "Be filled with the Spirit." "Grieve not the Spirit." These imply the self-control of the being who receives the command—*self-control in regard to, and under the influence of, the Spirit of God.*

The word and example of Christ are the guides,—the spirit is power prompting to speak and to do. It gives the impulse of life and love in the heart or sensibility, and through the emotions of conscience and love the will is influenced to obey Christ. Any one that claims to be wise above what is written, or to have received any *new revelation* from the Spirit, or to be filled with a spirit that produces *any other impulse than doing good to men,**—such claim in itself is evidence that the impression does not come from the Spirit of Christ.

The fanaticism of impulse, apart from revealed ruth, has been the bane by which Satan has abated the strength and impeded the progress of all great moral reformations. It marred and arrested the progress of the Lutheran Reformation on the Continent. The Wesleys labored wisely and earnestly to discriminate the vital doctrine of the Spirit from the delusive and emotional experiences which manifested themselves in some departments of their work. Jonathan Edwards wrote a treatise on the same subject; many of the Friends or Quakers erred in the same direction. It is the point where the holiest minds are sometimes tempted. This is exemplified in the temptation of the Saviour. When Christ overcame the temptations of the devil by trust in God, the next temptation was to lead the mind too far in the direction where it had experienced Divine favor; hence the temptation was, to pass from trust to presumption. Christ,

---

* See "God Revealed in Creation and in Christ." Book II, chap. 6.

as man's example, maintained His integrity by walking in the path of duty, *guided by a true application of Scripture*, which He quoted and applied to His circumstances.

William Penn saw the liability to error at this point, and frequently in his larger treatises, as in the lesser exposition of the Quaker tenets, states the correct doctrine of the Word and Spirit. In the tract called "Gospel Truths," he gives "a brief account of those things which are chiefly received and professed among us, the people called Quakers, according to the testimony of the Scriptures of truth, and the illumination of the Holy Ghost, *which are the double and agreeing record of true religion.*"

In the "General Epistle to the People of God" he says, "His word of light, grace, and truth in the heart, will cleanse the young man's ways, and guide the old man in the path he should walk to peace. I found that from the revelation of this word in the soul springs the true conviction and knowledge of God, and a man's self, and by nothing else can a man be convicted and born again."

In the tract, "Fiction Found Out," he briefly

enunciates his confession of faith. The first item is, "That the grace of God *within me*, and the Scriptures *without me*, are the foundation and declaration of my faith and religion, and let any man get better if he can."

F.

(Chap. VI, p. 105.)

VIEWS OF THE FIRST CHRISTIANS CONCERNING THE SECOND APPEARANCE OF CHRIST.

It is doubtful whether the apostles ever understood, as we may now, the relations of the promise in regard to Christ's second appearing.* The time of His appearing to destroy the temple, and with it the old dispensation, they did not definitely know, although they had intimations by which they might discern its approach, and prepare for the event (Heb. x, 25). But of the period of Christ's appearing to judge the world they had no knowledge, and the Saviour refused to give them even an intimation upon the subject, except that the papal apostacy would first rise and fall. Christ's coming and the end

---

* It was best, in many views of the subject, that this and some other non-essentials should not be fully developed in the first period.

of the world were events always associated in the minds of the disciples. When He had spoken to them of the certain destruction of the city and of the temple, affirming (Matt. xxiv, 2), "there shall not be one stone left upon another," the disciples inquire concerning two things specifically: (1) "Tell us when shall these things (the destruction of the temple) be; and (2), "What shall be the sign of Thy coming, and of the end of the world?" To these two questions Jesus answers. His answers are clear, although commentators generally confuse the sense. To the first, the destruction of the city, He answers, Matt. xxiv, from the 4th to the 29th verse, giving intimation of the approaching fall of Jerusalem, and indicating in the last verse of the passage that the city, which would be destroyed within the lifetime of some then living, would be overthrown by the Roman army.

From the 29th to the 31st verse He speaks of the general diffusion of the gospel through the known world by His disciples, who would be preserved in the fall of the city, and dispersed at the destruction of the Jewish state. The sun and stars are, throughout the Bible, the proper symbols for the ruling powers of a state. By the desolation and fall of these the disciples are taught that the Jewish state and rulers would be thrown down at the destruction of Jerusalem. The power of the old dispensation would cease; — then the power of the new dispensation would appear in progress — a progress to be accomplished by the dispersion of the Christians, who had been admonished to flee from Jerusalem, and probably from Judea, and who carried the gospel whithersoever they went.

Then, from the 32nd to the 35th verses, He tells them when they should see the natural indication of such events as those of which He had spoken; then, to be assured that the end of the Jewish state and dispensation was at hand, and to flee speedily from the coming destruction.

But in regard to the second question (or the second and third, if any choose to construe it in that sense) He answers with the same explicitness. They ask, secondly, "And what will be *the sign of thy coming, and of the end of the world?*"

To this, after answering the first, He replies from the 36th to the 46th verses, "*Of that day and that hour knoweth no man, no, not the angels of heaven, but my Father only.*"

He tells them that the latter period would come unexpectedly. That the duty in regard to that event was to watch and to work as a servant. That character, not outward circumstances, would be the criterion of safety (ver. 40, 41). He then, in the 25th chapter, gives the Parable of the Virgins, indicating an absence longer than was anticipated, and that, on account of the apparent delay, spirituality and watchfulness would abate in true Christians, and be lost by formalists. The Parable of the Talents follows, to show that the period was distant, but at the same time it was as near in one sense as the close of each man's probation. When each had used his talent in the absence of his Lord, then an account must be given, and judgment passed in view of the use of the talents intrusted to each individual. The passage closes with the final scene of the judgment, predicated on probation, in which He represents Himself as the *representative* of the suffering and the needy, and assures them that at His final advent men will be judged in view of the good they had done in His name to their fellow-men; and that He will receive good done to others as being done to Himself; and that their future destiny will depend upon a life-time of loving labor for the ignorant and the needy. He makes no event to intervene between probation and judgment.

There are different dispositions of the several verses by different evangelists, which may perplex the expositor,' but the outline and impression of the whole are the same. (1.) The place of the Jewish dispensation and state was to be destroyed *in that generation.* (2.) The dispersed Christians to preach, in time of distress, the gospel throughout the world. (3.) The time of the judgment at the end of the world unknown. (4.) Christ would be absent in person. A probation under the gospel would ensue, but during the long delay Christians would cease to watch, and sleep together with formal professors. But unexpectedly, at the end of personal probation, or at death, the Lord would come to reward the faithful, punish the unprofitable, and destroy those who rebelled against the reign of justice and love. It was therefore not only inexpedient, but it was merciful, in view of the circumstances of the early disciples, that the long period which was to intervene in time between the first and second personal advent should not be made known to them. It is difficult, in our present state, to connect the end of life and the end of the world together in the same motive; and yet, in both a practical and a spiritual sense, they are the same, albeit one be distant in time and the other near in eternity. All the actions upon which judgment is predicated close at death. As in a dream the sleepers are probably conscious of activity, of locality, of joy, while yet they may have no sense of time. Hence death and judgment, although temporarily distant, may be spiritually near.

All we can do in probation is limited by the end of life; and the motive to watch and to work is the same in both forms. Yet the kingdom of Christ, and Christ's personal coming at hand, have more of the spirit of faith and of immortality in them than the idea that the end of life is near. Hence it was no part of Christ's mission to reveal the judgment-period in any form. It was not revealed to the Son of Man, nor to the angels, but was known to the Father only. Therefore said Jesus to His inquiring disciples, even after His resurrection, "It is not for you to know the times or the seasons which the Father hath put in his own power." The true and the operative idea is to believe Christ's coming at hand. "After death the judgment."

But even after the outpouring of the Spirit, the question continued to be agitated. The first converts knew there were admonitions concerning watchfulness, flight, life, death, and judgment; and they did not discriminate between the end of the old dispensation, and that of the new. Scoffers,— probably apostates,— began to urge objections, and in some of the first churches there was anxiety in the minds of believers on the question of Christ's personal appearance. The people being thus interested and anxious, the apostles reply to the scoffers, present and prospective, on one hand, and to sincere inquirers on the other. They tell all they know in regard to the matter, and all that was necessary for the guidance of Christians in order to their sanctification.

To those who scoffed and said (2 Pet. iii), "Where is the promise of his coming, for since the Father fell asleep all things have continued as they were from the beginning of the creation?" the apostle answers in a form applicable to the past and present.

The same class of scoffers exist now, as then.

God, they say, instituted the laws of nature at the creation, He then withdrew. All things take place by law since the beginning, and therefore no divine interposition is possible. Peter replies, affirming that geological changes have taken place in the past, even to the destruction of the earth; and hence they may occur again. He affirms that the delay is in order to probation, that God desires to save some out of a selfish race; that the time, although long to us, is not long to God; but that the end will come; the judgment will sit, and God will destroy the wicked and the world together, and after the change there will ensue "new heavens and a new earth, in which shall dwell the righteous." Then, lest the notion of Christ at hand might lose force by his exposition, he closes his epistles by the faithful words, "Ye therefore, beloved, seeing ye know these things before, beware lest ye also, being led astray by the error of the wicked [that Christ will not come], fall from your own steadfastness.* But grow in grace, and in the knowledge of our

---

* Thus Christ's personal advent at hand was, as Gibbon alleges, made a motive to induce steadfastness in the apostolic age, as it has been at various periods down to our own time.

Lord and Saviour Jesus Christ. To him be glory both now and forever. Amen."

The Apostle Paul answers to those believers at Thessalonica, who were anxious in regard to this subject. In his first letter he had spoken of the final judgment (chap. iv, 13–18), and had described the hopes connected with the momentous event as a consolation to believers whose friends had deceased. He tells them to comfort themselves by these words; but immediately adds, — "But of the times and the seasons, brethren, ye have no need that I write unto you. For yourselves know perfectly that the day of the Lord so cometh as a thief in the night. For when they shall say, Peace and safety; then sudden destruction cometh upon them." These are the words of Christ repeated in the language of Paul.

But this church, probably by erroneous preaching and false spirits, was led to misconceive this language of the apostle in his first letter. He hears of this, and corrects their wrong impressions in his second. He tells them of further intimations which Christ had left with His apostles in regard to the same subject. He says there must come a great apostasy before the second coming of Christ. He then, in 2 Thess. iii, describes the Papal Apostasy in its most striking features, and says it must rise and reign and be destroyed before the second advent of the Redeemer, and closes, as the Apostle Peter has done, with an exhortation to steadfastness.* The apostasy spoken of has risen and reigned. In the Reformation, the judgment turned against it. Now God by His providence and His truth is "consuming and destroying it unto the end." All anti-Christian powers are in their decadence. Judgment, even to the seventh vial, is being inflicted upon every nation, state and church that refuses to make moral progress. The end is at hand. "Even so come Lord Jesus."

* Eph. vi, 6 — Heb. iv, 12.

G.

(Chap. VI, p. 115.)

BISHOP JEREMY TAYLOR ON THE EVIDENCE OF THE HOLY SPIRIT.

THE progress of *spiritual religion* has been but little furthered by the publication of many treatises on the evidences of Christianity; especially treatises on the *external* evidence, according to the manner of the eminent Dr. Chalmers. Such external evidences have their place, but it is not the place usually assigned them. They may aid the intellect in regard to an historical question; but it may be doubted whether they turn the attention of those most enlightened by them in a right direction. There is such a thing as the faith of men standing "in the wisdom of man and not in the power of God." Paul sought to avoid such a result in connection with his teaching. Treatises such as those of Erskine, Jenys, and others, showing that gospel principles are true in themselves, and in their adaptation to man's nature and wants, are of spiritual value, because they relate not to the letter but to the principles — the *spirit* and *practice* of the gospel. Yet, after all, there is a witness to the gospel accompanying the truth, and offered to all men who are willing to obey Christ. That witness is infallible. It is the "Spirit of Christ that is witness for us."

The following passages, on the subject of the true evidence of the Divine in our holy religion, are taken from the excellent treatise of Dr. Knox — "Christian Philosophy."

Opinions of Bishop Taylor respecting the Evidence of the Holy Spirit; "showing," as he expresses it, "how the scholars of the Universities shall become most learned and most useful."

"We have examined all ways, in our inquiries after religious truth, but one; all but God's way.* Let us, having missed in all the other, try this. Let us go to God for truth; for truth comes from God only. If we miss the truth, it

---

* See Bishop Taylor's "Via Intelligentiæ,"

is because we will not find it; for certain it is, that all the truth which God hath made necessary, He hath also made legible and plain; and if we will open our eyes we shall see the sun, and if 'we will walk in the light, we shall rejoice in the light.' Only let us withdraw the curtains, let us remove the impediments, and the sin that doth so easily beset us. That is God's way. Every man must, in his station, do that portion of duty which God requires of him, and then he shall be taught of God all that is fit for him to learn; there is no other way for him but this. The fear of the Lord is the beginning of wisdom; and a good understanding have all they that do thereafter. And so said David of himself: 'I have more understanding than my teachers; because I keep thy commandments.' And this is the only way which Christ has taught us. If you ask, 'What is truth?' you must not do as Pilate did, ask the question and then go away from Him that only can give you an answer; for as God is the Author of truth, so He is the Teacher of it, and the way to learn is this; for so saith our blessed Lord; 'If any man will do his will, he shall know of the doctrine whether it be of God or no.'

"This text is simple as truth itself, but greatly comprehensive, and contains a truth that alone will enable you to understand all mysteries, and to expound all prophecies, and to interpret all Scriptures, and to search into all secrets, all, I mean, which concern our happiness and our duty. It is plainly to be resolved into this proposition:

"The way to judge of religion is by doing our duty; and theology is rather a divine life than a divine knowledge.

"In heaven, indeed, we shall first see and then love; but here on earth we must first love, and love will open our eyes as well as our hearts, and we shall then see and perceive and understand.

"Every man understands more of religion by his affections than by his reason. It is not the wit of the man, but the spirit of the man; not so much his head as his heart that learns the divine philosophy.

"There is in every righteous man a new vital principle. The spirit of grace is the spirit of wisdom, and teaches us by secret inspirations, by proper arguments, by actual persuasions, by personal applications, by effects and energies; and as the soul of man is the cause of all his vital operations, so is the Spirit of God the life of that life, and the cause of all actions and productions spiritual; and the consequence of this is what St. John tells us of: 'Ye have received the unction from above, and that anointing teacheth you all things,'—all things of some one kind; that is, certainly all things that pertain to life and godliness: all that by which a man is wise and happy. Unless the soul have a new life put into it, unless there be a vital principle within, unless the Spirit of life be the informer of the spirit of the man, the word of God will be as dead in the operation as the body in its powers and possibilities.

"God's spirit does not destroy reason, but heightens it. God opens the heart and creates a new one, and without this creation, this new principle of life, we may hear the word of God, but we can never understand it; we hear the sound, but are never the better. Unless there be in our hearts a secret conviction by the Spirit of God, the gospel itself is a dead letter.

"Do we not see this by daily experience? Even those things which a good man and an evil man know they do not know both alike. An evil man knows that God is lovely, and that sin is of an evil and destructive nature, and when he is reproved he is convinced; and when he is observed he is ashamed; and when he has done he is unsatisfied; and when he pursues his sin, he does it in the dark. Tell him he shall die, and he sighs deeply, but he knows it as well as you. Proceed, and say that after death comes judgment, and the poor man believes and trembles; and yet, after all this, he runs to commit his sin with as certain an event and resolution as if he knew no argument against it.

"Now since, at the same time, we see other persons, not so learned, it may be, not so much versed in the Scriptures, yet they say a thing is good and lay hold of it. They believe glorious things of heaven, and they live accordingly, as men that believe themselves. What is the reason of this difference? They both read the Scriptures; they read and hear the same sermons; they have capable understandings; they both believe what they hear and what they read; and yet the event is vastly different. The reason is that which I am now speaking of: the one understands by one principle, the other by another; the one understands by nature, the other by grace; the one by human learning, the other by divine; the one reads the Scriptures without, and the other within; the one understands as a son of man, the other as a son of God; the one perceives by the proportions of the world, the other by the measures of the Spirit; the one understands by reason, the other by love; and therefore he does not only understand the sermons of the Spirit and perceive their meaning, but he pierces deeper, and knows the meaning of that meaning; that is, the secret of the Spirit, that which is spiritually discerned, that which gives life to the proposition and activity to the soul. And the reason is, that he hath a divine principle within him and a new understanding; that is, plainly, he hath love, and that is more than knowledge, as was rarely well observed by St. Paul: 'Knowledge puffeth up; but charity* edifieth;' that is, charity maketh the best scholars. No sermons can build you up a holy building to God unless the love of God be in your hearts, and purify your souls from all filthiness of the flesh and spirit.

"A good life is the best way to understand

---

* Ayann,—"Love of God."

wisdom and religion, because, by the experiences and relishes of religion, there is conveyed to them a sweetness to which all wicked men are strangers. There is in the things of God, to those who practice them, a deliciousness that makes us love them, and that love admits us into God's cabinet, and strangely clarifies the understanding by the purification of the heart. For when our reason is raised up by the Spirit of Christ, it is turned quickly into experience; when our faith relies upon the principles of Christ it is changed into vision; and so long as we know God only in the ways of men, by contentious learning, by arguing and dispute, we see nothing but the shadow of Him, and in that shadow we meet with many dark appearances, little certainty, and much conjecture; but when we know Him in the Spirit, and see Him with the eyes of holiness and the instruction of gracious experiences, with a quiet spirit and the peace of enjoyment, then we shall hear what we never heard, and see what our eyes never saw; then the mysteries of godliness shall be open unto us, and clear as the windows of the morning; and this is rarely well expressed by the apostle; 'If we stand up from the dead and awake from sleep, then Christ shall give us light.'

"For the Scriptures themselves are written by the Spirit of God, yet they are written within and without; and besides the light that shines upon the face of them, unless there be a light shining within our hearts, unfolding the leaves, and interpreting the mysterious sense of the Spirit, convincing our consciences and preaching to our hearts, to look for Christ in the leaves of the gospel is to look for the living among the dead. There is a life in them, but that life is, according to St. Paul's expression, 'hid with Christ in God,' and unless the Spirit of God draw it forth, we shall not be able.

"Human learning brings excellent ministries towards this; it is admirably useful for the reproof of heresies, for the detection of fallacies, for the letter of the Scriptures, for collateral testimonies, for exterior advantages; but there is something beyond this, that human learning without the addition of divine can never reach.

"A good man, though unlearned in secular knowledge, is like the windows of the temple, narrow without and broad within; he sees not so much of what profits not abroad, but whatsoever is within, and concerns religion and the glorifications of God, that he sees with a broad inspection; **but all** human learning with God is but blindness and folly. One man discourses of the sacrament, another receives Christ; one discourses for or against transubstantiation; but the good man feels himself to be changed, and so joined to Christ, that he only understands the true sense of transubstantiation, while he becomes to Christ bone of His bone, flesh of His flesh, and of the same spirit with his Lord.

"From holiness we have the best instruction. For that which we are taught by the Holy Spirit of God, this new nature, this vital principle within us, it is that which is worth our learning; not vain and empty, idle and insignificant notions, in which, when you have labored till your eyes are fixed in their orbs, and your flesh unfixed from its bones, you are no better and no wiser. If the Spirit of God be your Teacher, He will teach you such truths as will make you know and love God, and become like to Him, and enjoy Him for ever, by passing from similitude to union and eternal fruition.

"Too many scholars have lived upon air and empty notions for many ages past, and troubled themselves with tying and untying knots, like hypochondriacs in a fit of melancholy, thinking of nothings, and troubling themselves with nothings, and falling out about nothings, and being very wise and very learned in things that are not, and work not, and were never planted in Paradise by the finger of God. If the Spirit of God be our teacher, we shall learn to avoid evil and to do good, to be wise and to be holy, and to be profitable and careful; and they that walk in this way shall find more peace in their consciences, more skill in the Scriptures, more satisfaction in their doubts, than can be obtained by all the polemical and impertinent disputations of the world. The man that is wise, he that is conducted by the Spirit of God, knows better in what Christ's kingdom doth consist than to throw away his time and interest, his peace and safety,— for what? for religion? no; for the body of religion? not so much; for the garment of the body of religion? no, not for so much; but for the fringes of the garment of the body of religion; for such, and no better, are many religious disputes; things, or rather circumstances and manners of things, in which the soul and spirit are not at all concerned. The knowledge which comes from godliness is an unction from the Holy One — a something more certain and divine than all demonstrations and human learning.

"And now to conclude:— to you I speak, fathers and brethren, you who are, or intend to be, of the clergy; you see here the best compendium of your studies, the best alleviation of your labors, the truest method of wisdom. It is not by reading multitudes of books, but by studying the truth of God; it is not by laborious commentaries of the doctors that you can finish your work, but the exposition of the Spirit of God; it is not by the rules of metaphysics, but by the proportions of holiness; and when all books are read, and all arguments examined, and all authorities alleged, nothing can be found to be true that is unholy. The learning of the Fathers was more owing to their piety than their skill, more to God than to themselves. Those were the men that prevailed against error, because they lived according to truth. If ye walk in light, and live in the Spirit, your doctrines will be true, and that truth will prevail.

"I pray God to give you all grace to follow this wisdom, to study this learning, to labor for the understanding of godliness; so your time and your studies, your persons and your labors, will be holy and useful, sanctified and blessed, beneficial to men and pleasing to God, through Him who is the wisdom of the Father, who is made to all that love Him, wisdom, and righteousness, and sanctification, and redemption."

Will any one among our living theologists controvert the merits of Bishop Taylor? Is there one whom the public judgment will place on an equality with him? Will any one stigmatize him as an ignorant enthusiast? His strength of understanding and powers of reasoning are strikingly exhibited in his *Ductor Dubitantium*, in his Liberty of Prophesying, and in his polemical writings. I must conclude that he understood the Christian religion better than most of the sons of men; because, to abilities of the very first rank, he united in himself the finest feelings of devotion. His authority must have weight with all serious and humble inquirers into the subject of Christianity, and his authority strongly and repeatedly inculcates the opinion which I trust to maintain, that the best evidence of the truth of our religion is derived from the operation of the Holy Spirit on every heart which is disposed to receive it.

And I wish it to be duly attended to, that

the discourse from which the above extracts are made was not addressed to a popular assembly, but to the clergy of a university, and at a solemn visitation. The Bishop evidently wished that the doctrines which he taught might be disseminated among the people by the parochial clergy. They were disseminated; and in consequence of it Christianity flourished. They must be again disseminated by the bishops and all parochial clergy, if they sincerely wish to check the progress of infidelity. The minds of men must be impressed with the sense of an influential divinity in the Christian religion, or they will reject it for the morality of Socrates, Seneca, the modern philosophers, and all those plausible reasoners to whom this world and the "things which are seen" are the chief objects of their attention. The old divines taught and preached with wonderful efficacy, because they spoke as men having authority from the Holy Ghost, and not as the disputers of this world, proud of a little science, acquired from heathen writers in the cloisters of an academy. There was a celestial glory diffused round the pulpits of the old divines; and the hearers, struck with veneration, listened to the preacher as to an undoubted oracle. Full of grace were his lips; and moral truth was beautifully illuminated by divine. She easily won and firmly fixed the affections of men, clothed, as she was, with light as a garment.

Passages from the discourses of the celebrated Mr. John Smith, Fellow of Queen's College, Cambridge, corroborative of the opinion that the best Evidence of the Christian Religion arises from the energy of the Holy Spirit.*

"Divine truth is not to be discerned so much in a man's brain as in his heart. There is a divine and spiritual sense which alone is able to converse internally with the life and soul of divine truth, as mixing and uniting itself with it; while vulgar minds behold only the body and outside of it. Though in itself it be most intelligible, and such as the human mind may most easily apprehend, yet there is an incrustation, as the Hebrews call it, upon all corrupt minds, which hinders the lively taste and relish of it.

"The best acquaintance with religion is a

* See his Select Discourses.

knowledge taught of God; it is a light which descends from heaven, which alone is able to guide and conduct the souls of men to that heaven whence it comes. The Christian religion is an influx from God upon the minds of good men; and the great design of the gospel is to unite human nature to Divinity.

"The gospel is a mighty efflux and emanation of life and spirit, freely issuing forth from an omnipotent source of grace and love; that god-like, vital influence, by which the Divinity derives itself into the souls of men, enlivening and transforming them into its own likeness, and strongly imprinting upon them a copy of its own beauty and goodness: like the spiritual virtue of the heavens, which spreads itself freely upon the lower world, and subtly insinuating itself into this benumbed, feeble, earthly matter, begets life and motion in it; briefly, it is that whereby God comes to dwell in us, and we in Him.

"The apostle calls the law of ministration of the letter and of death, it being in itself but a dead letter, as all that which is without a man's soul must be; but on the other side, he calls the gospel, because of the intrinsical and vital administration of it in living impressions upon the souls of men, the 'ministration of the Spirit,' and the 'ministration of righteousness;' by which he can not mean the history of the gospel, or those *credenda* propounded to us to believe; for this would make the gospel itself as much an external thing as the law was; and so we see that the preaching Christ crucified was to the Jews a 'stumbling-block, and to the Greeks foolishness.' But indeed he means a *vital efflux* from God upon the souls of men, whereby they are made partakers of life and strength from Him.

"Though the history and outward communication of the gospel to us *in scriptis* is to be alway acknowledged as a special mercy and advantage, and certainly no less privilege to the Christians than it was to the Jews, to be the depositaries of the oracles of God, yet it is plain that the apostle, where he compares the law and the gospel, means something which is more than a piece of book-learning, or an historical narration of the free-love of God, in the several contrivances of it for the redemption of mankind.

"The evangelical or new law is an efflux of

life and power from God Himself, the original of life and power, and produceth life wherever it comes; and to this double dispensation of law and gospel does St. Paul clearly refer: 'You are the epistle of Christ ministered by us, written not with ink, but with the Spirit of the living God; not in tables of stone.'* Which last words are a plain gloss upon that mundane kind of administering the law, in a mere external way, to which he opposeth the gospel.

"The gospel is nòt so much a system and body of saving divinity, as the spirit and vital influence of it spreading itself over all the powers of men's souls, and quickening them into a divine life; it is not so properly a doctrine that is wrapt up in ink and paper, as it is *vitalis scientia*, a living impression made upon the soul and spirit. The gospel does not so much consist *in verbis* as *in virtute*;—in the written word, as in an internal energy."

* 2 Cor. iii, 3.

H.

(Chap. VI, p. 135.)

TESTIMONY AND PRAYER A NECESSARY ANTECEDENT TO MORAL PROGRESS IN THE WORLD.

THERE is a connection between providence and prayer which none but they who are spiritually-minded discern. The Christian, who sees the hand of God in human history, can deduce a law of Divine administration, which may be stated as follows : — The moral progress of the world is accomplished by the truth, uttered in the name of God, as a testimony against evil, and accompanied (as the testimony of true Christians always will be) by prayer.

The reasons of this law and the effect of its operation may be clearly discerned : — If there be moral progress it must be by the removal of moral evils ; but moral evils can be removed only by the reformation of the evil-doers, or by their destruction, or by the overthrow of the power by which they oppress or corrupt men. Hence, if states or churches do not repent when light is shed upon their evil principles or practices, their power must be broken, and the evil removed, by penalty upon the transgressors; because, as before said, the removal of the evil is necessary in order to the moral progress of the world; and there is no possible way of removing a moral evil but by the repentance of the subject, or by penalty upon him as a transgressor. So Jesus announces the principle in Matt. xxi, 33–43.

God sometimes permits an evil to exist for ages, as in the case of the papal superstition; while other combinations are going on fitting the world for the income of truth. The guilt of those who sin in darkness is, in one sense, overlooked; but when providence sends light it increases the guilt of those who resist it, hence their resistance fits them for more immediate penalty. "If I had not come and spoken unto them," said Christ, "they had not had sin, but now have they no cloak for their sins." "All things that are reproved are made manifest by the light; for whatsoever doth make manifest is light." That is, the moral evils in the minds or practices of men are shown to be such by the light of truth, and whatever reveals the moral evils of the world, and condemns them, is moral truth. Now, when the truth comes, men to whose practice it relates grow worse or better rapidly. They are called by providence to meet the moral issue presented in their times. Those who resist and cling to their evil, God makes blind by a law of their moral nature. They become morally insane in their attachment to their sin, and their evil passions rise against those who testify against it; and this state of mind is the unfailing antecedent of approaching doom. "Whom the gods would destroy they first make mad," is a maxim the pagan nations learned by experience. It is rendered in Christian theology by the apostle in 2 Thes. ii, 10–12, —" Because they received not the love of the truth, that they might be saved. For this reason God shall send them strong delusion that they might believe a lie: that they all might be damned who believed not the truth, but had pleasure in unrighteousness,"—*i. e.*, if men have pleasure in their sin instead of the truth which shows it to be sin, they will be blinded by their evil propensity, and fall under the Divine judgment.

The application of this principle in the moral progress of the world is plain. When an evil is to be removed, God sends light by His faithful witnesses; this places the evil doers in probation in regard to their bad principles and practices. They must either receive or reject the light. If they receive it, they repent and abandon their evil. If they reject it, they grow blind in regard to the guilt of their evil practices, and the evil is removed by overthrowing the power or destroying the influence of the evildoers. Thus, by one means or the other, or by both, God accomplishes the moral progress of the world. Whenever the witnesses have been moved by the Spirit to proclaim the truth with prayer in any country, and transgressors have rejected the truth, then will the end come by providential interposition.

Hence, after John and Jesus had given light, and the Jews as a nation had rejected it, they grew fanatical in their blindness, and their city and nation were destroyed. So old Rome—the gospel was preached in all her regions,—she rejected, persecuted the truth, and fell. So modern

Rome — during the dark ages she grew strong, and prospered in her superstition, because of the darkness, — when light came by the Reformation she rejected the light, and persecuted those who testified against her superstitions. Hence, since then one blow after another has fallen upon her, and she is now being " consumed and destroyed unto the end."

So in the slave states of America, — the reform which began in Great Britain was preached in America; the slave states, for the most part, rejected the truth, and retrograded into such moral blindness that they would now crucify the fathers of the Republic, whose tombs they built, if they were living, and dared to utter the sentiments in regard to slavery which they held in their life-time. The effect is moral blindness and insanity, and the end is as sure as the progress of time.*

The process, then, of moral progress in the

---

* Since this Appendix was written, the Rebellion in America has taken place. In our age penalty follows closely upon the rejection of truth. Slavery has fallen, as all minds in sympathy with God knew it must fall, and as the deduction in the above paragraph prophesied it would fall, after evil-doers had rejected the truth and were permitted to believe lies, in order that they might induce their own destruction.

world is,— first discussion, then agitation, then blindness increasing to moral insanity, on those who reject the light, then penalty upon the transgressors. The process may sometimes be slow, and sometimes rapid, but the end is sure. After truth comes fairly and fully into conflict with error, there is no peace to a wicked people.

We live in an age when truth is in conflict with error in every region of the world. In India, China, Turkey, the truth has been published; they have had time to hear and obey. Now these peoples are distracted by conflict, and their old forms are approaching dissolution. In such an age those states and churches which have accepted and maintained truth politically, socially, and religiously, will be in a great measure free from the agitations and evils which must come to those who maintain errors in government or religion. Wherever wrong or sin exists, the conflict of truth with the evil will produce agitation; while those where the truth exists in the greatest purity will be most peaceful and prosperous. Moral forces are the causes which are destroying evil; hence, when a church or nation is right, reason and conscience will not prompt agitation, but suppress it. When the natural and moral rights of man are recognized, the moral power of the human mind and the moral power of God, are engaged to defend, not to destroy, such a community.

Thus the true Church secures peace in every nation where her principles are accepted. The world does not know it, but it is true as inspiration, that the praying Church of Christ, which testifies against the evils existing in Church and State, is the saving health of a nation. No question can ever be finally settled until it is settled right, and hence peace can be gained permanently only by righteousness. The true Church does not war, but she proclaims the truth, resistance to which causes God to send war. The profane world — men without faith in God — look at the machinations of statesmen as the means of national prosperity and progress. There are some statesmen whose consciences are true, and whose efforts are sincerely devoted to the removal of evils in Church and State. But often public men get credit for doing what the advancing moral sentiment of the world renders it expedient for them to do. There is a power beyond and above public men that moves them, and surrounds and controls them, forcing them often to pursue a course which is better than their conscience, and which in other circumstances they would resist.*

Men and women whose consciences are adjusted and empowered by faith in gospel righteousness, and who *testify against whatever injures man*, are the conservators of peace and progress in a nation. Hence England, the non-slaveholding states of America, Switzerland, and other Protestant lands, will be peaceful and prosperous; or if they have conflict, the war will be without the gates. In the Reformation the judgment of providence turned against evil. The twelve hundred and sixty years of evil ascendency were fulfilled. Now, every struggle between light and darkness in every land will terminate sooner or later in favor of progress. We have reached the period in the world's moral history when the vials of divine wrath are being poured out upon evil churches and nations. The "harvest of the

---

* Witness the union of the old Whig party in the north, with the unmovable Anti-slavery men after the defeat of General Scott. Many of the old Whigs hated the Abolitionists, but their love of power was stronger than their hatred of wrong.

wicked" is being gathered. But the "wine-press of the wrath of God" will be trodden without the camp of the saints. Blessed is that people who hear, understand, and turn from the evil that hinders the progress of light and love in the earth.

I.

(Chap. VII, p. 137.)

IS PRAYER A FORCE IN THE MORAL WORLD?

PERSEVERING, *repeated*, *concentrated* thought in prayer is frequently enjoined in the New Testament by the words of Jesus. Prayer not only in behalf of the suppliant, as in the case of the importunate widow, Luke xviii, 1-8, but likewise in behalf of others, as in Luke xi, 5. Now God works in accordance with law in the spiritual world as in the natural. These injunctions therefore have their foundation in laws of mind, not yet perhaps well understood, but the existence of which should not be doubted. We can see, in part, reasons why answer to prayer in behalf of others is often delayed, and we can believe that such may often exist in the case of the suppliant himself.

Delay may be necessary in the *order of nature*. In order to responsibility there must be knowledge of duty; but religious knowledge is gained progressively, and this requires time. The will is influenced by motives. The evil of sin must be seen, the character of God considered, the beauty of holiness appreciated, but these require time; and furthermore presentation of motives usually depends on a second person, and on privileges and places — all of which require time.

Delay may be necessary in the *order of providence*. An individual may be so located in society that the truth and motive of the gospel can not reach him; or if they do, the hindering causes may be too great. But God converts and sanctifies by truth; hence, in order to an answer to prayer, Providence often removes individuals to some new locality, or arranges for them new surroundings, by which the effect of truth will be facilitated. But this requires time — often long years of time and effort.

But especially delay is necessay in *the order of love*. God always labors to reform before He executes penalty, "not willing that any should perish." The long suffering of God waits and works for the individual by reason, by motive, by providence, by Spirit: hence answers to prayer for others, even in cases where their selfishness is not desperate, may be long delayed. Where there is truth in the mind, and surroundings favorable, the work of the Spirit may be immediate, in other cases the order of time, providence, and love may require delay.

We know that there is always efficiency in the prayer of faith offered by an obedient Christian, but we do not know enough to affirm the *modus operandi* of that efficiency. It is thought by many who have investigated the subject without prejudice, that there is sufficient evidence to prove the existence of a law of mind, the formula of which is, — that *strong mental desire, if it carries with it a strong purpose of will in regard to another, does often affect the mind of the object upon whom the urgent mental effort is concentrated.*

The writer has not sufficient knowledge either to affirm or deny on the question of the existence of such a law. But if there be a law that can be expressed by this or by any similar formula, then it is easy to see that *the concentrated struggle of desire and will in prayer*, which the Scriptures require, without giving a reason, has an import that comes in some way under the universal category of cause and effect. And when such moral influence is accumulated by united prayer, and by prayer *the impulse and direction of which is given by the Holy Spirit*, while some may doubt whether there be such a law, others will see that the Divine impulse thus added to the human desire would make a law of itself.

Subsequently to writing the matter and the notes of the preceding sections, the author received and read with great interest the volume entitled "Müller's Life of Trust." The churches need such a testimony in our own times. The experiences of such saints as Knox, Fox, Woolman and Franke are almost forgotten. It is interesting to find a living illustration confirming the power of prayer by the attainment of beneficent objects before the face of this unbelieving age; and although the form of Mr. Müller's faith can not be expected by all persons in all circumstances, yet with Mr. Müller's impulses, and in the providential circumstances in which he has acted, his "*faith in the living God*" is that of the true Christian, and the results are an illustration of the omnipresence and faithfulness of Christ, which will refresh believing minds.

K.

(Chap. VII, p. 143.)

OLD AND NEW TESTAMENT MORALITY.

To believe and obey God as He makes Himself known to us by revelation, is the essence of all religion. And in all dispensations, from the patriarchal, with little more than the light of nature, down to the perfect in Christ Jesus, faith is the same principle working by love to the character and conformity to the will of God —so far as God reveals Himself. Abraham, who in the darkness of his age needed to be taught that human sacrifices were not required, exercised faith as truly as Paul. And by his faith he was willing to trust and sacrifice all of earth to the will of God. Hence examples of faith in the Old Testament are for all ages, while examples of morality are defective if viewed in the light of the New Testament. Many well-meaning men have hindered progress and perverted conscience by endeavoring to make the Old Testament morality coincide with the New Testament precept, and *vice versa*. This is contrary to the repeated and express teaching of the inspired writers. Old Testament saints would, in many leading instances, be New Testament sinners. Men may apologize for slavery, concubinage, prevarication, and various other immoralities, by Old Testament example. It seems almost as difficult to detach the Church in the modern age from the limited, introductory system of Moses, as it was in the days of Paul. It was "well for the early Christians to take heed to the light shining in a dark place, until the day dawned and the day-star arose in their hearts;" but after the New Testament dispensation had been established, then the first "had no glory by reason of the glory that excelleth." (See Epis. to Heb. *passim*.)

Still, persons who "have their senses exercised by reason of use," will be able to discriminate the kernel from the husk in all dispensations. There is a province where the scholarly beneficiaries of religious establishments and the preaching machines produced by many seminaries in modern times, may exercise themselves, and have in some cases as much truth on their side in regard to the letter of revelation as the dogmatic defenders of the faith. But so long as the spirit and precepts of the gospel are self-evidently perfect and ultimate; so long as faith in Christ crucified produces humility and labor for human good; so long as the Christian faith works by love and purifies the heart from sin; so long as the promise of the Spirit may be consciously known in experience; so long as these and other essential things are in the gospel, and are apparent to all who have eyes to see, the good man, while he will appreciate well-designed efforts for science or for sect, has a duty devolved upon him for Christ and his fellow-men which is above these, and which includes all sciences and all sects.

There is a province in which those who are in the line of legal ordination, and who labor in the *letter* and in truth, may be more useful than those who contend for forms rather than for faith. If they would devote attention to portions of Scripture that are poetical illustrations, which have been construed as historical statements—such, for instance, as quotations from the book of Jasher—or to those passages which have been a chief source of skeptical objections, but which do not belong to Holy Scripture, or are of doubtful authority, such as the destruction of Saul's posterity by David; and the closing verses of the gospel by Mark; the fourth verse of the fifth chapter of John, and other similar passages;—or if they would pay some attention to those who allegorize and spiritualize Solomon's Song, or the common histories of Jewish institutions or Jewish individuals which have been compiled in the Old Testament, they would accomplish a work favorable to the progress of truth, and acceptable to many who love our Lord Jesus Christ better than they do themselves.

PUBLISHED BY S. C. GRIGGS & CO., CHICAGO.

A Work of Great Interest to Clergymen, Lawyers, Teachers, and all Public Speakers.

A Manual of Gesture,

WITH OVER 100 FIGURES,

Embracing a Complete System of Notation, together with the Principles of Interpretation, and Selections for Practice.

BY ALBERT M. BACON, A.M.,
Professor of Elocution.

260 pages. - - - - - - - Price, $1.75

Prof. William Russell, the eminent Elocutionist of New England: "Your Manual is so thoroughly practical, and so carefully condensed, that it must be an invaluable aid to every faithful student of true eloquence. No one who consults your compend for his personal guidance can form a false or inappropriate style of action, whether as regards popular or professional oratory, and the study which receives the union of true art and the grace of cultivated nature."

B. C. Davis, Prof. of Elocution, Union Christian College, Ind.: "Admirably adapted to students first beginning the study, as well as to the most advanced."

Rev. Edward Lounsbery, President of Griswold College, Iowa: "His system is very simple and natural; his interpretation exceedingly beautiful and effective."

The Chicago Pulpit: "It seems expressly arranged for the help of those who study alone, and have undertaken self-instruction in the art of persuasive delivery. We think that the work in the hands of our ministry, well studied, would have the effect of emphasizing the living words of the gospel all over the land, and making them two-edged with meaning."

The United Presbyterian, Pittsburgh: "It is thoroughly practical, and its few general principles easily understood. Over 100 figures help to understand the rules for gesticulation. They will be of use to any speaker, and help to overcome bad habits, whilst to the young student they will be invaluable from the start."

To be had of Booksellers, or sent by mail, postage paid, on receipt of $1.75 by the Publishers,

S. C. GRIGGS & CO.,
Chicago.

PUBLISHED BY S. C. GRIGGS & CO., CHICAGO.

"Indispensable to every public or private library worthy of the name."—*The Christian Intelligencer, New York.*

PRE-HISTORIC RACES
OF THE
UNITED STATES.

BY J. W. FOSTER, LL.D.,
Author of "The Physical Geography of the Mississippi Valley."

415 pages, crown 8vo., with a large number of Illustrations, engraved expressly for the work. - Price, $3.50

CONTENTS.

CHAPTER I.—The Antiquity of Man—Evidences in Europe.
CHAPTER II.—The Antiquity of Man—Evidences in the United States.
CHAPTER III.—The Mound-Builders—The Geographical Distribution of their Works.
CHAPTER IV.—Shell Banks—Their Geographical Distribution.
CHAPTER V.—Mounds and Enclosures.
CHAPTER VI.—The Mound-Builders—Their Arts and Manufactures.
CHAPTER VII.—Ancient Mining by the Mound-Builders.
CHAPTER VIII.—Crania of the Mound-Builders.
CHAPTER IX.—Manners and Customs as the Basis of Ethnic Relations.
CHAPTER X.—Who were the Mound-Builders?
CHAPTER XI.—The Unity of the Human Race.
CHAPTER XII.—Chronometric Measurements as Applied to the Antiquity of Man.   Appendix; Index.

"A careful examination of the book has satisfied us that it is one of the most interesting and important contributions to American archæology that have yet appeared, and will take rank among the leading treatises upon the general subject by European archæologists.

"We had thought of making some extracts from the volume, but it is so full of interest, from beginning to end, as to make selection perplexing; and were it not for the restraints of copyright we should be tempted to run the whole work through the *Popular Science Monthly*, as it contains just the kind of information, in clear, compressed, and intelligible form, which is adapted to the mass of readers. * * The whole exposition is condensed into 400 pages, and the publishers have done their part, in the fine execution of the engravings, and the beautiful typography of the book."—*The Popular Science Monthly, New York.*

For sale by the Booksellers, or will be sent, postage paid, on receipt of price by the Publishers,

S. C. GRIGGS & CO.,
Chicago.

PUBLISHED BY S. C. GRIGGS & CO., CHICAGO.

"The man who can secure a wide reading for this volume will do an amount of good second only to that done by him who wrote it."—*Northwestern Christian Advocate.*

Getting On in the World;

OR, HINTS ON SUCCESS IN LIFE.

By WILLIAM MATHEWS, LL.D.,
Prof. of Rhetoric and English Literature, University of Chicago.

"**Beautifully printed, and handsomely bound**" in cloth. - $2.25

Rev. Noah Porter, D.D., LL.D., *Pres't of Yale College:* "A book in which there is abundant matter of great interest."

Hon. Henry W. Paine, LL.D., *Boston, Mass.:* "Have read it through, not only with great interest, but possibly, late as it is, with some profit. Had I fallen in with this book forty years ago, it would have saved me FROM MANY SERIOUS MISTAKES AND THE LOSS OF MUCH TIME. * * You have written an admirable book. It cannot fail to do good. It ought to be in the hands of all young men, and especially of all young scholars."

Rev. J. M. Gregory, LL.D., *President of Illinois Industrial University:* "It is one of the best books of the class that I have ever seen. It fills me with a sort of wonder by its wealth of incident and appropriate anecdote. * * The book is eminently wholesome; it is more—it is a tonic of the most vigorous sort, and I shall advise all of our young men to read it."

Edwin P. Whipple, Esq., *the distinguished critic, in the Boston Globe:* * * "The present volume of Prof. Mathews indicates the nicety and the extent of his English studies, in the richness and variety of his quotations. His subjects are eminently practical, and he treats them in a practical way; but then what wealth of illustration he brings in from English poets, dramatists, divines, lawyers, and jurists! The anecdotes alone of the book should make it popular."

Rev. Dr. Curry, *Professor of English Literature, Richmond College, Va.* (in the *Religious Herald*): "Prof. Mathews has given us a book of rare interest. We have read it with delight and profit. The style is clear and charming. The subjects are eminently practical. The pertinent illustrations show a wide and careful reading. This volume places the author among the *best English essayists.* The young man who reads this volume will have his pulse quickened, his moral vision clarified, his faith and purpose strengthened."

Sold by all Booksellers, or will be sent, post-paid, on receipt of price by the publishers.

PUBLISHED BY S. C. GRIGGS & CO., CHICAGO.

OLD-TIME PICTURES
AND
SHEAVES OF RHYME.
By BENJ. F. TAYLOR.

Red Line Edition, Small Quarto, Silk Cloth, Plain, - $1.75
The Same, Full Gilt Edges, - - - - - - - 2.00

"The opening poem gives name to the book. It is thrilling in its interest and more elaborate than Mr. Taylor's usual scintillations. * * IT BURNS WITH THE WHITE HEAT OF GENIUS. * * There is a wide circle of readers who greatly admire Mr. Taylor's inimitable style, and will eagerly welcome this beautiful volume. One's blood tingles as one reads his 'Cavalry Charge,' 'Atlantic, 'Decoration Day, and several other soul-stirring rhymes. The pathos of 'The Isle of the Long Ago,' and 'The Dead Grenadier,' is intense. Humor often blends with the pathetic, laughter and tears alternating. HIS IMAGINATION GLOWS WITH DIAMONDS AND THE DICTION IS EXQUISITE."— *Evening Journal, Chicago.*

"All worthy of the head and heart of their gifted author."— *Albany Evening Journal.*

DRAMATIC STORIES,
FOR
HOME AND SCHOOL ENTERTAINMENT.
BY LAVINIA HOWE PHELPS.

12mo., 262 pages. - - - - - - - Price, $1.50

CONTAINS TWENTY-FIVE PLAYS.

"They are easy of representation, the incidents are healthful, the language strong and pure, and the general design advantageous alike to actor and listener."— *Boston Commonwealth.*

Sold by the Booksellers, or sent, postage paid, on receipt of price by the publishers,

S. C. GRIGGS & CO.,
Chicago.

www.ingramcontent.com/pod-product-compliance
Lightning Source LLC
Chambersburg PA
CBHW021345230426
43666CB00006B/420